To Do Justice and Right Upon the Earth

Papers from the Virgil Michel Symposium on Liturgy and Social Justice

Rosemary Haughton
Eugene A. LaVerdiere, S.S.S.
William Skudlarek, O.S.B.
R. Kevin Seasoltz, O.S.B.
Stanley M. Hauerwas
Regina Wentzel Wolfe
Daniel Rush Finn
Bernard F. Evans

Mary E. Stamps
Editor

A Liturgical Press Book

THE LITURGICAL PRESS
Collegeville, Minnesota

To
Don E. Saliers
for whom worship is a powerful art

BX
1970
.A1
V53
1993

Cover design by Fred Petters

Copyright © 1993 by The Order of St. Benedict, Inc., Collegeville, Minnesota. All rights reserved. No part of this book may be reproduced in any form or by any means, electronic or mechanical, including photocopying, recording, taping, or any retrieval system, without the written permission of The Liturgical Press, Collegeville, Minnesota 56321. Printed in the United States of America.

1   2   3   4   5   6   7   8

Library of Congress Cataloging-in-Publication Data

Virgil Michel Symposium on Liturgy and Social Justice.
  To do justice and right upon the Earth : papers from the Virgil Michel Symposium on Liturgy and Social Justice / Rosemary Haughton . . . [et al.] ; Mary E. Stamps, editor.
     p.   cm.
  Includes bibliographical references and index.
  ISBN 0-8146-2167-8
  1. Catholic Church—Liturgy—Congresses. 2. Christianity and justice—Catholic Church—Congresses. 3. Christian ethics—Catholic authors—Congresses. 4. Catholic Church—Doctrines—Congresses. 5. Social justice—Congresses. I. Haughton, Rosemary. II. Stamps, Mary E. III. Title.
BX1970.A1V53   1993
261.8—dc20   93-2448
                                                                          CIP

Contents

Foreword v

About the Authors vii

1 The Spirituality of Social Justice 1
  Rosemary Haughton

2 Worship and Ethical Responsibility in the Bible 16
  Eugene LaVerdiere, S.S.S.

3 Preaching and Social Justice:
  The Lectionary and the Persian Gulf War 33
  William Skudlarek, O.S.B.

4 Liturgy and Social Consciousness 41
  R. Kevin Seasoltz, O.S.B.

5 In Praise of *Centesimus Annus* 63
  Stanley M. Hauerwas

6 The Ethical Imperative of the Eucharist:
  Responding in the Workplace 84
  Regina Wentzel Wolfe

7 Poverty and Prosperity in Global Economics:
  Making Sense of Conflicting Claims 96
  Daniel Rush Finn

8 God's Creation and the Christian's Response 106
  Bernard F. Evans

Foreword

It is impossible to remain individualistic in prayer and sincerely social in daily life, or to remain individualistic in daily life and become sincerely social in prayer.

These words ring as true today as they did when Virgil Michel[1] wrote them over a half century ago. They remind us that the seemingly disparate aspects of our existence—our work, play, and worship, our relationship with God and our relationships with other human beings and with the created order—are in reality threads woven together to form a single fabric. They remind us that we are made for each another.

The essays in this book explore the linkage between social life and social prayer as embodied in the Eucharist. They were selected from a series of papers delivered at the Virgil Michel Symposium[2] in honor of the one hundredth anniversary of Pope Leo XIII's encyclical *Rerum novarum*. This landmark document addressed the problems brought about in society by the industrial revolution. It is widely considered to be the beginning of Roman Catholic social teaching. In fact, *Rerum novarum* set the stage for such influential papal documents as *Quadragesimo anno*, *Pacem in terris* and *Centesimus annus*.

Each of the authors writing in this volume is an heir to the spiritual and ethical legacy of these encyclicals. For them, the paschal mystery of the Eucharist is intrinsically formative of a genuinely Christian vision of society, although they approach the subject from perspectives as widely varied as prayer and proclamation, Scripture and ethics, worship and work, economics and ecology. Through their words we may gain deeper insight into the necessary connection between liturgy and justice, that is, between how we worship and how we serve. Just as Pope Leo XIII offered a cogent response of faith to the historical conditions of his day, so we too are compelled by participation in the liturgy to a common vision of peace with justice in our day. To be worthy of the name "Christian," we must become sincerely social in prayer as well as in our daily lives.

I would like to thank Fr. Dale Launderville, O.S.B., dean of the school of theology and rector of St. John's Seminary in Collegeville, and The Liturgical Press, who entrusted me with the task of editing this book. I am also grateful to those faithful persons who have by their example deeply influenced my own understanding of the inextricable ties between social justice and social prayer: the students, staff, and faculty of the Candler School of Theology and University Worship communities at Emory University, Rev. W. T. Horst, Rev. Evelyn Durkee, and the congregation of the First United Methodist Church of St. Cloud, Minnesota, the Benedictine communities of St. John's Abbey and St. Benedict's Convent, and my dear friends Allen and Marsha Bryan in whose company I have heard the voice of God calling.

Mary E. Stamps

Notes

[1] Virgil Michel, O.S.B. (1890–1938), was a Benedictine of St. John's Abbey and a leader in the American liturgical movement.

[2] The symposium was held at St. John's University, Collegeville, Minnesota, in July 1991.

About the Authors

Bernard F. Evans, holder of the Virgil Michel Ecumenical Chair in Rural Social Ministries at the school of theology, St. John's University (Collegeville, Minnesota), has published articles on environmental ethics and Christian stewardship in *Worship, The Catholic World, USA Today* and *The American Land Forum*. He is co-editor of *Theology of the Land* (The Liturgical Press, 1987).

Daniel Rush Finn is both an economist and a theologian and has written and lectured widely on the relation of ethics and economics. He is a member of the school of theology faculty and holds the William E. and Virginia Clemens Chair in Economics and the Liberal Arts at St. John's University (Collegeville, Minnesota).

Stanley M. Hauerwas is professor of theological ethics at the divinity school of Duke University and currently serves as the director of the graduate program in religion. His most recent books are *After Christendom* (Abingdon), *Naming the Silences: God, Medicine, and the Problem of Evil* (Eerdmans), and *Resident Aliens* (Abingdon), co-authored with William H. Willimon. He taught for fourteen years at the University of Notre Dame and has published on Catholic moral theology.

Rosemary Haughton is a theologian who has authored thirty-five books and received six honorary degrees. The mother of ten children, she is a member of Wellspring House, a community committed to the provision of shelter for homeless families and to the development of innovative projects for low-income housing. Among her best-known books are *The Transformation of Man* (1968), *The Catholic Thing* (1978), *The Passionate God* (1980), *The Re-Creation of Eve* (1985), and *Song in a Strange Land* (1990).

Eugene A. LaVerdiere, S.S.S., a holder of the Margaret and Chester Paluch Chair of Theology at Mundelein Seminary, University of St. Mary of the Lake, Mundelein, Illinois (1990–1993), is the senior editor of *Emmanuel* magazine and an adjunct professor of New Testament studies at both Catholic Theological Union, Chicago, and Mundelein Seminary. He is the consultant for mission education of clergy and seminarians for the national office of The Society for the Propagation of the Faith. Father

LaVerdiere is the author of many books, articles, and cassettes, both audio and video.

R. Kevin Seasoltz, O.S.B., a monk of St. John's Abbey in Collegeville, Minnesota, teaches sacramental theology in the school of theology of St. John's University, is a past rector of St. John's Seminary and the editor of *Worship*.

William Skudlarek, O.S.B., of St. John's Abbey is an associate professor of homiletics in the school of theology, St. John's University, Collegeville, Minnesota. He spent five years as a Maryknoll Associate doing missionary work in Brazil. He is the author of *The Word in Worship: Preaching in a Liturgical Context* (Abingdon, 1981).

Regina Wentzel Wolfe, holds a visiting appointment at Loyola University, Chicago. She has worked in market and economic research in the United States and Hong Kong and was an assistant editor for *The Tablet*.

1
The Spirituality of Social Justice[1]

Rosemary Haughton

Introduction

The more I think about spirituality and social justice, the more I am reminded of the kind of spirituality I learned as a very young convert to Catholicism, which taught me how I could "sanctify" my everyday occupations by uttering ejaculations—hundreds of them, if possible—and also by taking set times for meditation before or in between work times. I even bought a breviary and plodded through the Latin office, determined to be as "spiritual" as possible. I joined the Young Christian Students, the English equivalent of the French Jeunesse Etudiante Chretienne, which was the student effort to keep up with the energy and enthusiasm of the Jeunesse Ouvriere Chretienne, the Young Christian Workers. Some of us studied the gospels and the social encyclicals with amazement and a sense of huge possibility. We sang songs and argued with young Communists; all of this laid a foundation for lay-leadership structures which would be strong enough to support the Church through the worst of the storms which were to follow the Second Vatican Council. In celebrating the centenary of *Rerum novarum* now, we are touching back into that time when the social encyclicals were reclaimed with hope by a generation of energetic young Catholics. If a large part of this leadership structure proved, in the end, not to be weatherproof in the storms which followed, and was either wrecked or had to be demolished, still a great deal was learned. Significant was the flaw which offered as spirituality to enthusiastic and dedicated people a condensed and watered down version of monastic discipline. It was a spirituality which had to be *added* to the justice work in which we were involved, as a protection against the dreaded disease of activism. This was spirituality *and* social justice—with constant reminders of the primacy of spiritual things and the hope—sometimes quite explicit—that this experience would induce young people to "go the whole way," as it was expressed, and become priests and religious.

This kind of dualism, however unintended, will not do. But if one were to change the little word "and" to "of," the whole picture would change. I had an interesting experience, recently, of what happens when "of" is put into the phrase. I work in an organization, Wellspring House, which provides shelter for homeless families, is involved in creating affordable housing, and in providing education. In the course of ten years, about two hundred families have passed through the family shelter. Two years ago, the Board of Directors of Wellspring House decided to research what happens to homeless families after they settle into permanent homes: What difference did their experience of homelessness make? What was happening in their lives? Were they working? Were they at school? Were they still on welfare? What about their children? What were their goals and their dreams? Although research of this kind had not been undertaken before, we felt it was necessary in order to provide a realistic foundation for future projects or programs to meet the needs of these families and other poor families.

To present the results of the research, we decided to hold a symposium, not only to receive the report and study it but also to build upon it in order to create some action plans, and to ask for commitment to the process of carrying out social changes in the local area. One unusual thing about this symposium was that it was structured towards radical and practical future projects. It was also unusual that among the over one hundred people attending the two-day event—including people from business, education, churches, media, and politics—there were twenty formerly homeless women, most of whom had been part of the research process, three of whom had graduated from college the day before the symposium and one who had refused a planned celebration of her graduation in order to attend. A third unusual aspect was that the focus of the symposium was on the power of imagination as a tool of social transformation, through an address and guided process led by a woman whose doctoral dissertation had been on this subject, and who had cofounded and developed a successful grass-roots educational project for poor women outside Dublin in Ireland. The combination of these three unusual features was what created the explosion of energy and hope which was a true experience of the spirituality *of* social justice.

Some people were uncomfortable with the process for precisely that reason. There was laughter over amazing pictorial visions of what the local area might be like in future years. There were women with inadequate education raising issues, proposing possibilities, and generally being heard. There was a crossing of lines of class, gender, education, and race; there were flowers and songs. To a few, it was all shockingly unprofessional. There were mutters about "feminists," meaning any women who had clear opinions and stated them, and about the "not real world," meaning that the gathering was proposing not to accept the myths which assign to the "have-nots" silence and guilt, and to the "haves" power and all the decision making.

However, the mutters were drowned out, not merely by high spirits but more importantly by a persuasive combination of seriousness and hope. Liberated by the permission to imagine something different, minds and hearts were focused on practical steps towards possibilities which conventional wisdom denied or would not even consider. The sight and sound of women with histories of abuse and rejection, not long since traumatized by the humiliation of homelessness and the welfare system, now claiming leadership, interacting with assurance and friendship with people from totally different backgrounds, was in itself a profound spiritual experience.

Scripture and the Spirituality of Social Justice

This experience clarified for me, personally, the way in which spirituality—the movement and power of divine life itself—depends on the willingness of human beings to allow that power to be rooted in specific human and social situations. Without this rootedness, spirituality is in danger of being merely a concept, a feeling, or a personal search doomed to frustration because it seeks in the wrong place.

Ben Sirach, writer of the Book of Ecclesiasticus, a person full of shrewd worldly wisdom on how to prosper in an oppressive and unjust society, also understood that men and women grasp at wisdom for sheer survival. In this book—and in other Wisdom literature—there is nothing that one could call a spirituality of social justice but there emerges, paradoxically, a sense of what such a concept could mean. Wisdom, in Ben Sirach, will help people to survive, although he has no expectation that the structure of society itself could be inspired by it; but, in spite of social injustice—which is a given—he sees Wisdom as a social phenomenon rooted in the common life of a particular people. He wrote at a time when the vision of universal social justice and peace proclaimed by the great prophets had perhaps already been transposed into an otherworldly or eschatological hope, if there was hope at all. However, it is helpful to us as we struggle to recover from a similarly spiritualized, yet basically cynical, dualism to realize that in such a situation Wisdom might still be perceived as a community-based phenomenon—even if her chief beneficiaries were to be individual persons who are prepared to accept a personal discipline rejected by a majority intent on wealth and success.

In the famous passage in which Wisdom proclaims her own praises, Ben Sirach describes her as a divine emanation, an agent of creation, present in the depths and the heights, holding power over all things. Yet the divine power remains, in a sense, ineffective, unless she can be rooted in place and time, in a given human society. Wisdom is commanded to "make your home in Jacob and find your heritage in Israel." Once she has "taken root" among the beloved people, she is able to grow and flourish, and to bear fruit—that is, Wisdom's accessibility to human beings. "Come to me, you who desire me, and eat your fill of my fruit—to obey me is to be safe from disgrace, those who work in Wisdom will not go astray" (Sir 24:19, 22).

So wisdom becomes practically available in the community, and only in the community. Wisdom is identified elsewhere as the Torah, the source of wise behavior and attitudes in the community, the means of covenant obedience and salvation. This concept is helpful in the process of developing a spirituality of social justice, precisely because it does *not* envisage what we would regard as social transformation. Wisdom, in this view, is God's gift, and available to all, even though clearly she does not prevail, or the survival skills preached by the sage would not be necessary. Yet, the manifest beauty and generosity of divine wisdom as she grows, and even the shifts and struggles of the wise person trying to cope with folly, convey the feeling that there should be more to life than personal rectitude and avoidance of trouble—what might be called a spirituality of survival—though that is no mean feat in any culture.

It is in the prophets, whose wholistic vision was already lost when Ben Sirach wrote, that we can perceive the emergence of what might be called a spirituality of social justice, for their passionate denunciations of oppression and their soaring visions of a transformed society assume that divine power works primarily in the people as a whole. Ben Sirach taught a kind of bourgeois adjustment to a so-called reality with which we are very familiar. But the prophetic tradition, existing in one form or another from the time of the early monarchs until after the exile, consistently evoked a possible and accessible situation in which God would be free to interact with the people, who are then able to be prosperous and happy with their God and with one another. Thus the basis of prophetic denunciations, whether addressed to individual kings, to priests and officials, or to the nation as a whole, is the fact that callousness, greed, and power-seeking have frustrated God's will to dwell among the people in a society of peace and plenty.

The social justice character of prophetic spirituality is demonstrated in a special way in a passage from Jeremiah in which, out of the overwhelming grief he personally feels at the horrors which are already engulfing his people, he asserts the need for what might be called a pedagogy of mourning. Sin and the horror are so pervasive, the guilty and innocent so inextricably intertwined in the results of generations of cynical injustice and oppression, that the prophet knows it is not enough for himself or a few exceptional people to bewail the evil. National disgrace and disaster require national repentance if any kind of healing is ever to happen. So Jeremiah calls on the professional mourners, the "women skilled in keening" to take on the work of grieving, not for individual bereavement but for the sake of the whole people threatened with dying. He calls on the women to lead the mourning process, and so to enable others also to grieve. These teachers of grieving will liberate the necessary sorrow, breaking down barriers of apathy or despair "that our eyes may run with tears and our eyelids be wet with weeping." Jeremiah is clear that this is a skill to be learned, and that the source of it is God. "Listen, you women, to the words of Yahweh, that your ears may catch what God says," because that is how they will be able to initiate a true process of social regeneration. But it will take time, and so the women must also "teach your daughters the lament, let them teach one another the dirge" (Jer 9:20). And so, in the end, God will be able to "do justice and right upon the earth." This spirituality of social justice will require a commitment to the work of denunciation and grieving and is founded on an accurate social analysis. Jeremiah knew not only what was wrong but also why it had happened.

In the Synoptic Gospels we discover that Jesus had also taken on this prophetic task of denunciation and grieving. Like Jeremiah, his awareness of the need for this work was also based on a social analysis, expressed in biting and uncompromising terms.

Jesus denounced a practice of religion which side-stepped the demands of justice and so maintained the poor in a carefully organized state of paralysis and debilitating guilt. He stood in the tradition of Deutero-Isaiah, the prophet of the community returned from exile which was already engaged in rebuilding a theocracy interpreted by a religious elite at the expense of the poor.

Fasting and religious practice which are intended to express solidarity with the poor are self-contradictory, says the prophet, when they are accompanied by injustice over subordinates. Fasting means letting go—letting go of superiority, indifference, and unjust power. When these are let go, then God's light will break out of you, and you will grow like a watered garden. And, interestingly, "you will be called Rebuilder of broken walls, Restorer of houses in ruins" (Sir 49:13). The edifice of justice is the community in which Wisdom dwells; it is not new, its design is ancient, but it must be rebuilt over and over again.

When Jesus called the poor to himself, promised them a burden easy to bear, poured out on them forgiveness, healing, and hope, he was not offering a dualistic salvation which would heal them individually and spiritually while leaving untouched the causes of their misery. He was proclaiming the reign of God as the community of justice and peace in which all systems of alienation—whether of race, gender, or religious role—would be dismantled.

Call no one "father," if father means power and control over others' lives. Serve one another, take the lowest place, socialize with what you thought were your social inferiors, reverse your ideas about who is in and who is out, as far as God is concerned. This is the same vision proclaimed by Deutero-Isaiah of a new heaven and a new earth, in which people would live long and at peace, build houses and live in them, grow food and eat it, and in which children would live to grow up. Echoes of the more usual experiences are poignant in this passage. As we look around, we recognize just how amazing this vision is, apparently so simple. For we, in our time, also see people building by their labor a society that denies them decent housing and the ability to afford to eat the food they grow and process. So, in the prophet's words, they raise children for misfortune, because that is how we expect things to be. "And my people will have it so," says Jeremiah. But it does not have to be like that and, until things change, God is hidden; God is on the other side of a gap, and access to God is controlled by those who have good reason to fear what would happen if God were to be set free. The whole earthly career of Jesus was one long struggle to persuade people that God was extremely accessible, that there was, in fact, no gap except in the guilt-ridden imagination of religious systems. Because people found it virtually impossible to accept such an idea, they were always trying to set limits to God's freedom—maybe unto seven times. It was—and is—hard for any society to accept this because accessibility of God means being accessible to each other; it means social justice, the dismantling of oppressive systems on which, in practice, our prestige and our lifestyle depend. Social justice is one name for the reign of God. Spirituality of social justice is the quality of divine-human relationship which the prophets envisioned and Jesus announced, and for which they lived and died.

From the great prophets, and from Jesus as inheritor and crown of the prophetic tradition, we have this spirituality which is rooted in the human community, yet is penetrated through and through with divine presence and dynamism. The key concept which makes us aware of this is the promise that "before they call I will answer, and while they are still speaking I will listen!" In the prophetic vision of human life there is, from God's point of view, no gap between divine and human, no lapse between petition and fulfillment, because the movement of hope and effort in the human community is the movement of divine energy itself. This is the fullness of the spirituality of social justice.

Liberating Symbols, Seeking Social Justice

The great question we are left with, therefore, has to do with our own need to close, or at least narrow, the dualistic gap between spirituality and social justice. At a certain practical level it has to do with such questions as how to avoid burnout, how to be compassionate without being destroyed, how to be politically active without being co-opted by evil systems, how to live with the fact that, intentionally or not, we are all enmeshed in and dependent on evil systems which feed us, educate us, and even subsidize our efforts to mitigate their destructive effects!

An emphasis upon considering the relationship between liturgy and social justice is important, because a dualistic gap exists in the area of liturgy; the thrust of social justice as spirituality comes right up against liturgy and what that represents. I want to conclude by reflecting on the roots of what might be called the social injustice of liturgy, and through that to indicate how we might begin to work at closing the gap which we experience, as people committed to social justice in the tradition of Jesus and the prophets.

When I use the phrase "the social injustice of liturgy," I am referring to a very basic experience in the major denominations, whether in the Catholic, Reformed, or Eastern Orthodox traditions: the fact that access to the experience of community rituals of major spiritual significance is controlled and exercised by the same elite groups who also hold—or at least claim—the power to interpret the whole religious tradition, the consciences and behavior of believers, through their regulation of morality, spirituality, and theology. This is so normal to us that we seldom question it or even think about it. Yet the prophetic criticism of Jesus, and of the prophets before him, was provoked by precisely this kind of experience—that the religious establishment exploited the deep desire of the people to experience the divine, in order to maintain control over them for their own profit. And profit in this sense does not mean merely financial gain (though it depends on that for its continued existence); it has even more to do with the need for power. What happened in the time of Jesus, and has been happening ever since, is that the basic human need for mystical and spiritual experience, especially through powerful symbolic ritual, is exploited in order to impose the kind of theology and codes of morality which serve to uphold the ecclesial power structure—which, in its turn, dictates the form of the ritual for its own purposes. Thus social injustice, in the form of a closed and self-perpetuating system of religious control, is built into the liturgical experience.

It is not surprising, then, that it is possible for regular and sincere church-goers to accept instances of pervasive social injustice—in this country alone, a rising tide of child-poverty, the normative abuse of women, the deliberate creation of an underclass—as irrelevant to the practice of religion, and even to the pursuit of holiness. As the spirituality of the Gospel is privatized and cut off from its prophetic roots, liturgical experience is deprived of its power. Divine Wisdom is denied her deep roots in the community and must survive in an ecclesiastical greenhouse, the key to which is carefully guarded.

Ritual—a great, deep, and powerful ritual, gathered around age-old and universal symbols—is a necessity for the life of the human spirit; it is a communal experience, even as it is also a profoundly personal one. As with vitamins, people are not necesssarily aware that they are suffering from a vitamin deficiency, but they just feel listless and tired, and are vulnerable to disease. Similarly, people suffering from a ritual deficiency are spiritually tired and lacking in energy, they wonder what has happened to their spiritual energy, they find it hard to resist the attacks of persuasive doctrines such as those of the cults or the market place, because there is such a spiritual apathy in their lives.

This is a real dilemma. I am suggesting that it may be at the heart of our search for a spirituality of social justice. To cultivate a deep personal spirituality and engage with others in works of justice (whether as a career, job, or in spare time), to give money and thought and energy in response to the Gospel mandate, is very hard if there is no place in daily life where one can be nourished by the fruit of divine Wisdom, or respond to the call to share her bread and her wine which grow from the ground of community in which God is perceived to dwell.

There is a de facto separation between the source of symbolic ritual, controlled and adapted as it is to the needs of the religious establishment, and a life of prophetic commitment to social justice. Most people learn to live with this. They shop around and try to find what they call "a good liturgy," or they grab such crumbs of nourishment as they can from what is offered. They compensate for their continuing hunger through prayer-groups and Bible study groups, which may evolve their own modest rituals. More and more people, in time, look for ways to create rituals that draw on the symbols and the great traditions, but in ways and forms that express the common search for a whole spirituality. What we need is a way to liberate ritual so that it can become a deep spring for our spirituality of social justice. The great visions of the prophet, the lived vision of Jesus, which was experienced by his immediate followers, and the indwelling of divine wisdom, have to find some form of expression which is ritual and communal.

Walter Brueggemann wrote in *Prophetic Imagination* about the work of the prophet in breaking through what he calls "dissatisfied coping"[2] in the face of fears of change which would mean loss of control for the establishment. "Dissatisfied coping" describes very well the experience of many religious people, whether in sixth century Judah or twentieth century America. Brueggemann suggests that an essential element in cutting through that dissatisfaction is the offering of symbols—symbols, he says,

> that are adequate to contradict a situation of hopelessness in which newness is unthinkable. . . . the prophet is to provide the wherewithal whereby hope becomes possible again to a community of kings who now despair of their royalty. After a time kings become illiterate in the language of hope. Hope requires a very careful symbolization.[3]

But Brueggemann is clear that we cannot invent new symbols. "Rather," he says,

> it means to move back into the deepest memories of the community and activate those very symbols that have always been the basis for contradicting the regnant consciousness. . . . And when the prophet returns, with the community, to those deep symbols, they will discern that hope is not a late, tacked on

hypothesis to save a crisis, but rather the primal dimension of every memory of this community.[4]

Such a hope, released through the experience of basic communal symbols, is the hope of social justice, because social justice is simply our way of talking about the character of a society in which God lives and acts freely, a thing impossible in situations of oppression. When injustice—which requires constant lying, hypocrisy, and denial for its survival—reigns, then no human relations can be healthy, and no community can be spiritual; the only possible gods are idols.

Our search for a spirituality of social justice requires that we liberate the symbols that have been co-opted to be tools of oppression. We must dare to engage in ritual in a way that touches hope and to perceive the deep roots of our symbols, the roots of divine Wisdom. Then we need to discern what is authentic in the rituals and what has been co-opted, and to recognize with joy that hope and reality can break out of even a co-opted ritual, which is, of course, why it can survive; it *does* nourish us, but not enough for full health.

I must say that I do not know how this work of discernment, remembering, and activation of symbols is to be done. I know that, in some ways, it *is* being done, simply because so many people of faith are aware of this gap which is a source of profound spiritual weakness. The spirituality of social justice can never be the transforming power that it should be unless it finds full ritual expression; so the work being done to bridge the gap, even in small groups and in modest and unobtrusive ways, is deeply important.

However, there is one aspect of the search for a more authentic ritual which is very obvious. It seems to me inescapable that the lack of authenticity in much public ritual is profoundly connected to the exclusion of women, not just in the sense of refusing ordination to women—some major churches do ordain women and so far it has not made much difference to the availability of ritual as a source of social empowerment—but in the sense that ritual in our churches is tied to a patriarchal system in which the perpetuation of male control is the central issue.

I am not suggesting that we could solve this simply by putting ritual in the hands of women. We are all in this together. Women and men have all internalized the patriarchal "angst": a distrust of the symbols unless they are controlled and sanitized, the fear that divine Wisdom might get out of hand if given too much room, and also the fear of looking foolish. What I am suggesting is that a spirituality of social justice has to be concerned, probably before anything else, with the issue of sexism, of the normative patriarchal fear of the feminine and the consequent oppression and abuse of women. Unless we are working at the roots of this injustice, we will never release the power of the spirit in our churches. Oppression of woman is central not because it is worse than oppression based on race, age, or health, but because women represent the essential "other" which our culture fears, the fearful "other" which we do not understand or do not admit, and which is personified in those who look different, sound different, or dress differently. It is this "otherness," evoking the power of the symbols of night and earth, of birth and death, which women especially embody. But this is the dangerous power beyond our control which makes transformation possible.

I said that I am not speaking only or even mainly of the refusal to ordain women, because the issue is much broader than that, though it includes it. But I do have a memory connected with this which illuminates the way in which the significance of the great symbols can be changed, challenged, and can release power, if the feminine element in it is allowed to become clear.

A few years ago a friend and I were asked to conduct a one-day retreat on a Saturday for about fifty people in an Episcopal parish. The retreat closed with a liturgy of the now familiar informal kind, which was fun, friendly, and participative. It made no particular impression on me, except to put me in touch once more with the sense of something missing. The next day we were invited to take part in the main Sunday liturgy of the parish, which was a full and formal Eucharistic celebration in the old Prayerbook form, with organ, choir, and incense. Having been brought up an Anglican, I have an affection for this familiar ritual, now four hundred years old, but the experience was transformed for me by one circumstance: when the procession approached the altar the celebrant, fully vested in a magnificent chasuble, was seen to be a woman; she was pregnant and near her term. My experience of that liturgy had very little to do with feeling happy that a woman was able to perform this sacred function, but it had everything to do with the entirely unforeseen way in which her presence at the heart of this very traditional ritual transformed the quality and meaning of the symbols. Here was a woman bringing the message of Christ to those who wait, a woman dispensing forgiveness and healing hurts, a woman feeding the little ones of God, a woman handling vessels of nourishment, and afterwards washing them. In one way, it all seemed so obviously natural. These are, traditionally, feminine functions, which does not mean that only women can do them, but does mean that we need to release the basic human and feminine power of our symbols.

To confine to one sex in a cultic context the functions usually confined to the other sex in the secular context amounts to a spiritual lobotomy. Like a lobotomy, it is an operation designed to reduce to passive manageability a personality whose behavior is unacceptably disturbing and bizarre. (Unacceptable to whom?) But this is what has been done to the collective personality of the worshiping church. So we gain a well-behaved, predictable congregation, and lose the power of imagination, the prophetic rage, the visionary energy. I do not really like the implications of that image, because it seems to mean that there is no way that the spirituality of social justice can discover its fullness in the context of this kind of Christian religious behavior permitted within the major Churches—or the minor ones, for that matter. You cannot reverse a lobotomy. But, after all, we are not talking about a single personality. The image is a strong warning, but it also forces us to realize that there are things going on in the Churches which are not in the prayer-books and missals, which are not taught in seminaries or included in parish bulletins. There is prophecy going on, ritual going on, and mysticism going on. People are living a spirituality of social justice without quite knowing it, simply by supporting each other in a struggle, resistance, and faithfulness to the gospel. Men and women are discovering the reality of shared discipleship, but it costs them dearly.

There are no easy answers. The Church is where we discover the shoots of divine Wisdom and even her fruits. The Church is where she is betrayed and confined. The Church bears the tradition and buries it. The Church is liberator and oppressor. Each of us, separately and yet never without each other, has to work out a way to draw from the roots, to stand in the tradition, to be freed by the symbolic power of such ritual as we can discover. Each of us bears the responsibility for the future Church so that it can grow into the fullness of its real calling and let go the deadness of unreality.

The best way I can evoke that possibility is to recall the hideously bizarre image used many years ago in the novel by Walter Miller, Jr., about a future period beyond nuclear devastation, *A Canticle for Leibowitz*.[5] It is the the story of civilization on the other side of a nuclear holocaust which reduced it to its primitive beginnings, has managed since then to repeat all the sins and errors of pre-nuclear western history, and has once more reached a point of inevitable nuclear destruction. As the bombs are about to fall, a woman comes to make her confession to a priest. She is one of the long-term effects of the earlier long-ago nuclear destruction, a mutant with two heads, one of which, apparently that of a young girl, never speaks but seems to sleep on her shoulder. The bomb falls as the old woman, enduring the evil with a peasant shrewdness, is making her confession; the priest leaves her and rushes to take the Sacrament from the tabernacle before the church falls. As he leaves, he is half crushed by the falling masonry—symbolically by the sheer weight of the church. In his dying, half lucid state he becomes aware of a figure kneeling near him, the figure of a woman with two heads; but it is the young head which has awoken, and the dying priest, in the ruins of the church, is offered communion from the spilled Sacrament at the hands of this woman just coming to life out of the body whose old head now hangs, dead, on her shoulder. The woman bears the possibility of newness; she is new, without a father, nurtured by the old body until the time when destruction released her. Virgin-born, immaculate, she takes water and baptizes herself. In whatever future there may be, she makes a slow, amazed effort to speak a new language. In it she can convey pardon to the man to whom her old self had turned for absolution.

This is an ambiguous image, as all good images are. Perhaps the fullness of spirituality can only be released by the death of the old; yet the mere possibility of the new is carried and nurtured in the dying, wise, sinful body of the old.

Can we discover a true and unambiguous spirituality of social justice? Probably never completely. We live out our calling in ambiguity, obliged to use old language to stammer out the phrases of a whole new awareness. We must use the skills and methods of mammon, the secular or the religious version, to do the work of God. We push at the limits of available structure, available rite, available words, which never seem quite able to express what we see or half-see, hear or half-hear, perhaps. Grasping at the always elusive, which we know is there, is the penalty of prophecy, which is the reason why prophets, including Jesus, have frequently been deemed to be crazy and a danger to society. Our Churches are always liable to feel, as the family of Jesus did, that we should be restricted for our own good. Or, we may end up with Jeremiah in a cistern. But the cistern is perhaps the place where divine Wisdom draws water for her garden. There are worse vocations than to be the water with which Wisdom makes paradise grow.

Notes

[1] This essay has also been published in *Sisters Today* (November 1991).

[2] Walter Brueggemann, *The Prophetic Imagination* (Philadelphia: Fortress, 1978) 65.

[3] Brueggemann, 66.

[4] Brueggemann, 66.

[5] Walter M. Miller, Jr., *A Canticle for Leibowitz* (Philadelphia: Lippincott, 1960) 315–317.

2
Worship and Ethical Responsibility in the Bible

Eugene LaVerdiere, S.S.S.

Worship demands ethical responsibility. It was so in Old Testament times and it was so in New Testament times. Worship calls for a set of ethical responses, and apart from these responses, worship has no value.

What are the grounds for so close a relationship between worship and ethical responsibility? What demands does worship place on the worshippers? How does it affect their relationships? Do the two Testaments differ in these matters? My purpose is to explore these questions, which are as important today as they were in biblical times. What is at stake is the value of our own worship.

Is it not something that we are able to celebrate Eucharist and see no connection between what we do there and the way we treat our neighbors, our colleagues, or even our own family?

Is it not amazing that a wealthy parish can celebrate Eucharist and give little or no thought to the homeless all around it or even to the neighboring parish hopelessly mired in poverty?

And is it not something that we can gather at the table of the one who is Lord of all and continue to ignore racist policies and attitudes in the workplace or marketplace and even in our own office?

And again is it not amazing that Roman Catholic airmen can go straight from Mass to a bombing raid with little or no concern for fellow Catholics on the receiving end, let alone for human beings of another faith?

Not that we are without prophetic voices. In the past year (1990–1991) the Holy Father himself spoke out very clearly, over and over again, praying and pleading that the allies not go to war in the Middle East.

There are other prophets too: Dom Helder Camara, tireless in his denunciation of institutionalized poverty, Mother Teresa of Calcutta, reaching out to those most abandoned by the rest of society, and many others, in all parts of the world. We applaud them. We honor them. We pray for them. But we do not listen to them.

It is as though a wall had been erected between the liturgical and the ethical, effectively sealing one off from the other and leaving the liturgy with no formative influence on people's lives. A liturgy sapped of ethical challenge makes little difference for Christian living. Ultimately, severed from life, its emptiness shows through, and it becomes very boring.

The present state of things, sad as it may be in an age of renewal, is not cause for discouragement. It may always have been like this. The disassociation of ethics from worship seems to be as old as original sin. It was certainly the case in biblical times. But this is no reason for complacency, as even a short sampling of prophetic texts shows. We have much to learn from our ancestors in the faith.

Prophetic Appeals

Recall first the voice of Isaiah confronting Judah, whose worship had lost both meaning and value because of the people's disregard for the moral law:

> What care I for the number of your sacrifices?
>   says the Lord.
> I have had enough of whole-burnt rams
>   and fat of fatlings;
> In the blood of calves, lambs and goats
>   I find no pleasure. . . .
> When you spread out your hands,
>   I close my eyes to you;
> Though you pray the more,
>   I will not listen.
> Your hands are full of blood!

> Wash yourselves clean!
>> Put away your misdeeds from before my eyes;
> Cease doing evil;
>> learn to do good.
> Make justice your aim:
>> redress the wronged,
> hear the orphan's plea,
>> defend the widow (Isa 1:11, 15-17).

The people of Judah came to offer sacrifices and prayers with hands dipped in the blood of oppression and injustice. Their worship left them unconcerned for their own poor and helpless. Because of this, their sacrifices became worthless and even offensive to God. Isaiah could not have been more clear. Worship demanded concern for one's fellow Israelites, especially those whose only human recourse was the community.

In the matter of worship and ethical responsibility, no one spoke out more strongly than the prophet Amos:

> I hate, I spurn your feasts,
>> I take no pleasure in your solemnities;
> Your cereal offerings I will not accept,
>> nor consider your stall-fed peace offerings.
> Away with your noisy songs!
>> I will not listen to the melodies of
>> your harps.
> But if you would offer me holocausts,
>> then let justice surge like water,
>> and goodness like an unfailing stream (Amos 5:21-24).

Israel substituted worship for faithful adherence to the covenant and its laws. It offered sacrifices, but bereft of justice and goodness, its worship had become repulsive to God. Amos' message found an echo in Hosea:

> For it is love that I desire, not sacrifice,
>> and knowledge of God rather than holocausts (Hos 6:6).

Isaiah had emphasized the need for purification, doing good, redressing the wronged and defending the helpless. Amos had stressed the need for justice and goodness. Hosea asked for love and knowledge of God. For Micah it was a matter of doing what was right, loving goodness and walking humbly with God:

> With what shall I come before the Lord,
>   and bow before God most high?
> Shall I come before him with holocausts,
>   with calves a year old?
> Will the Lord be pleased with thousands of rams,
>   with myriad streams of oil?
> Shall I give my first-born for my crime,
>   the fruit of my body for the sin of my soul?
> You have been told, O man, what is good,
>   and what the Lord requires of you:
> Only to do the right and to love goodness,
>   and to walk humbly with your God (Mic 6:6-8).

All of these prophetic texts address situations in which the ethical sphere was divorced from the liturgical. The Israelite prophets clearly saw that worship demands ethical responsibility and did all they could to associate one with the other. So did the Psalms, calling for worship in spirit and truth and for a clean heart to offer true sacrifice. Sacrifices must be accompanied by right living:

> Consider this, you who forget God,
>   lest I rend you and there be no one to rescue you.
> He that offers praise as a sacrifice glorifies me;
>   and to him that goes the right way
>   I will show the salvation of God (Ps 50:22-23).

For those who have offended God, sacrifices must also be accompanied by humility and sincere contrition:

> Free me from blood guilt, O God, my saving God;
>   then my tongue shall revel in your justice.
> O Lord, open my lips,
>   and my mouth shall proclaim your praise.
> For you are not pleased with sacrifices;
>   should I offer a holocaust,
>   you would not accept it.
> My sacrifice, O God, is a contrite spirit;
>   a heart contrite and humbled, O God,
>   you will not spurn (Ps 51:16-19).

Then consider Paul, the best known of our New Testament prophets, addressing the situation at Corinth, barely five years after its first evangelization:

> When you meet in one place, then, it is not to eat the Lord's supper, for in eating, each one goes ahead with his own supper, and one goes hungry while another gets drunk. Do you not have houses in which you can eat and drink? Or do you show contempt for the church of God and make those who have nothing feel ashamed? What can I say to you? Shall I praise you? In this matter I do not praise you (1 Cor 11:20-22).

Many of the Corinthians who gathered for the Lord's Supper disregarded not only the poor at large but even those who belonged to their community and gathered with them to eat the Lord's Supper. Because of this, the Lord's Supper at Corinth was a sham. What was meant to be the Lord's Supper was turned into each one's private supper. The Christian assembly became pointless. It would have been better for the Christians to stay home.

Read in isolation, Paul's statement may seem somewhat extreme, but not when we compare it with the prophetic texts we have just read from the Old Testament.

Paul called the Christians at Corinth to a way of life and a set of attitudes that were consistent with the Lord's Supper. Apart from this way of life, there could be no Lord's Supper. The prophets had a similar message for Judah and Israel. Moral life that was not consistent with their worship made their worship worthless and even repugnant to God. Like the Lord's Supper at Corinth, worship remained such only in name.

The texts just cited are very clear. In the nature of things, there is a close relationship between worship and ethics, between prayer and sacrifice and the way we treat our neighbor. But what are the grounds for this relationship? And are they identical in both Testaments? Those are the questions that are addressed later in the essay.

First, I shall offer some reflections on worship and ethical responsibility in the Israelite context. For this, I shall focus on the biblical theme of the covenant, recognized as one of the most pervasive in the Hebrew Bible.

Second, I shall offer some reflections on the Christian assembly for the Lord's Supper and its relationship to ethical responsibility.

For this, I shall focus on the meaning and implications of the name Lord's Supper.

Worship and Ethical Responsibility in the Mosaic Covenant

The covenant is a literary theme, intimately associated with the entire Bible. It is also a religious theme with ramifications for every aspect of Israelite life. And it is a reality, a reality of grace through which the Israelite tribes were gathered and maintained as a people of God. The covenant also provided the context for worship and the grounds for ethical responsibility.

Literarily, the covenant theme permeated the entire Bible. The Law told the story of the covenant's background in Genesis and that of its origins and early history from Exodus to Deuteronomy. The prophets called the people to fidelity to the covenant, and in effect to their own story. The Psalms were the prayerful response of the covenanted people to the Lord of the covenant. Wisdom literature showed how one lives concretely in the context of covenant faith.

As a religious reality, the covenant consisted in a set of relationships whereby each Israelite belonged to a people chosen to be God's people. Its origins lay in a great liberating act of God, who brought the Israelites out of Egypt and led them through a formative desert experience into the promised land. The covenant and its story were the basis for understanding every aspect of life.

Israelite worship was that of God's covenanted people. It was offered in recognition of Israel's debt of gratitude for its liberation from oppression and God's gift to it of the covenant of peace. A debt of gratitude is very special. Unlike a debt of justice, it can never be repaid. That means the need to offer worship can never be satisfied.

The covenant included a code of laws, which constituted its conditions. From the beginning, as we read in Exodus 19 to 24, Israel committed itself to observe the laws faithfully. Observance of the laws demonstrated their adherence to the covenant God offered them. By offering the covenant, God showed that he was with them. Fidelity to its laws showed that they were with God.

The covenant also provided the grounds for Israel's ethical responsibility. As we can see from the text of the decalogue in Exodus 20 and Deuteronomy 5, the laws of the covenant dealt with Israel's relationship to God, including its expression in worship. They also dealt with the Israelites' relationships with one another. For this people, ethics, morality, and the whole range of their dealings with one another were inseparable from the way they dealt with God, whether in personal prayer or in public worship.

Ethical responsibility flowed from the people's relationship to one another in the context of the covenant with God. Their ethics were basically one of response, as we see from the introduction to the decalogue: "I am the Lord your God, who brought you out of the land of Egypt, out of the house of slavery; you shall have no other gods before me" (Exod 20:2-3; see also Deut 5:1-6, 15). How God's people dealt with other members of God's people was part of their response to God's saving presence to them. Ethical responsibility, like worship, flowed from Israel's debt of gratitude. As in the case of worship, that debt could not be repaid. The people of the covenant could never be absolved of their ethical responsibility. In the world of the biblical covenant, we are very far indeed from the individualistic attitudes toward worship that are so prevalent in the modern world.

The covenant was a historical event that involved a particular people and its special relationship to God. The worship that was part of life in the covenant also involved a particular people, not the universality of the human race. Since worship flows from life, those who were outside the covenant event and did not share in its life did not participate in its worship. Today we would tend to call such worship exclusive, but this was quite understandable in light of Israel's need to maintain its religious identity while surrounded by people with different forms of religion.

The ethical responsibility that flowed from covenant worship was also exclusive. Those who accepted the conditions of the covenant accepted responsibility for their neighbor, that is for others who belonged to the covenant and shared life with them (see Lev 19:17-18). The covenant did something tremendous. It broke down the ancient tribalism and gathered the tribes into one people with common concerns. That was wonderful for those who formed part of that people. There would be no more intertribal wars. But what of all those other peoples and tribes who remained outside the Israelite covenant?

There lies a great limitation in the ethical responsibility that flowed from covenant worship. It did not extend to the whole human race but only to one's neighbor in the covenant. This limitation helps to explain ancient Israel's war ethics in the occupation and settlement of the promised land, where repeatedly we read of how Israel slaughtered entire populations, including the women and the children. Those who were slaughtered did not belong to the covenant people. They were not considered to be one's neighbor.

The limitation, however, was not absolute. From the beginning there was one great exception. Israel's ethical responsibility did extend to the resident alien or sojourner (*gēr* in the Hebrew Bible; *prosēlutos* in the Septuagint). Sojourners always remained sojourners. But in some way, while not being Israelite or belonging fully to the covenant, the sojourner or resident alien was affected by the covenant and subject to some of its laws.

Witness, for example, this legal text from Exodus regarding sabbath observance:

> But the seventh day is the sabbath of the Lord, your God. No work may be done then either by you, or your son or daughter, or your male or female slave, or your beast, or by the alien who lives with you (Exod 20:10).

The basis for this extension of the law to the resident alien lies not in the covenant but in the divine act of creation, which extended to all human beings. This is indicated in the verse immediately following the one just cited:

> In six days the Lord made the heavens and the earth, the sea and all that is in them; but on the seventh day he rested. That is why the Lord has blessed the sabbath and made it holy (Exod 20:11).

Resident aliens were not only subject to certain laws. They were also the object of the Israelite's ethical responsibility. "You shall not molest or oppress an alien," states Exodus 22:20, "for you were once aliens yourselves in the land of Egypt."

The same basis in Israel's historical experience in Egypt—a pre-covenant experience—is provided in Leviticus 19 as part of a rich blend of cultic and ethical obligations:

> When an alien resides with you in your land, do not molest him. You shall treat the alien who resides with you no differently than the natives born among you; have the same love for him as for yourself; for you too were once aliens in the land of Egypt. I, the Lord, am your God (Lev 19:33-34).

The text includes a positive admonition as well as a negative prohibition: It is not merely that one must not wrong or oppress the resident alien; one must love the alien as oneself. One must view the alien as one who is native born.

From Leviticus 19:33-34 we might conclude that being a resident alien is tantamount to being one of God's people, especially when we recall Psalm 146:9, announcing that

> The Lord protects strangers (Hebrew, *gērim;* LXX, *prosēlutous*);
> the fatherless and the widow he sustains,
> but the way of the wicked he thwarts.

However, the resident alien never becomes fully integrated into those referred to as neighbor. This is clear from an earlier injunction from Leviticus 19:

> You shall not bear hatred for your brother in your heart. Though you may have to reprove your fellow man, do not incur sin because of him. Take no revenge and cherish no grudge against your fellow countrymen. You shall love your neighbor as yourself. I am the Lord (Lev 19:17-18).

In this text the neighbor is clearly limited to someone who belongs to the Israelite people, "your fellow countrymen." It does not include the resident alien. Hence the need for a parallel statement extending the law of love to the resident alien:

> You shall love your neighbor as yourself;
> have the same love for him [the alien] as for yourself
> (Lev 19:18, 34).

While ethical responsibility that sprung from covenant worship is quite limited, it is not altogether exclusive. It does extend to the resident alien in Israel's midst. The basis for this extension is twofold: the event of creation and Israel's pre-covenant life as an alien in Egypt. This may appear as a fairly small concession, but it is an opening to the universality associated with creation and with Israel's role vis-à-vis the nations as spelled out, for example, in Isaiah 42, where God's concern extends to everyone who breathes and where Israel, we are told, was given the covenant that it might be a light to the nations (see vv. 5-7).

Worship and Ethical Responsibility in the New Testament

The same universality characterizes both worship and ethical responsibility in the New Testament, where the covenant and belonging to the people of God are open to all human beings.

The political and social situation in which Jesus of Nazareth taught and in which the Church was born was extremely different from the one addressed by the Old Testament. Part of the change was related to Israel's political status. Israel had lost its independence and was part of a vast empire whose central government was far away at Rome. The Jews were governed at first by a prefect and later by a procurator appointed by Rome, which kept a close eye on Palestine and Judea through the governor of Syria, whose capital was Antioch.

In this new context the Jews themselves had become resident aliens in a land dominated by foreigners. It consequently made very little sense for them to refer to the foreigners as resident aliens, and they certainly did not apply the term to themselves. The old term *prosēlutos* did remain in use, however, but with an entirely new meaning.

We learn from the New Testament (see Matt 23:15; Acts 2:11; 6:5; 13:43) that "proselyte" (*prosēlutos*) no longer referred to resident aliens but to converts to Judaism, those who identified with Judaism, accepted its laws and observances, were circumcised, and became members of the synagogue. In the Old Testament *prosēlutos* referred to one who received special consideration but never actually became a member of the people of God. In the New Testament it refers to one who becomes fully integrated into the Jewish people.

This change in the status of the alien was accompanied by a major shift in perception regarding who constituted the neighbor. The question "Who is my neighbor?" no longer hinged on the status of the resident alien but on that of the greater world in which Israel was immersed.

We have an echo of this shift in a dialogue between Jesus and a Levite on how one inherits eternal life. When Jesus asked about the law in this matter, the Levite recalled the commandment of love:

> You shall love the Lord, your God with all your heart, with all your being, with all your strength, and with all your mind, and your neighbor as yourself (Luke 10:27).

Wishing to justify himself, we are told, the Levite then raised the question, "And who is my neighbor?" (Luke 10:29). Jesus responded by telling a story about a good Samaritan and urging the Levite to imitate the Samaritan's behavior. In the Old Testament, especially when Israel enjoyed full independence, the Levite's question would not have arisen. However, when Israel lost its independence and became part of the Roman Empire, it became an important issue. For Jesus, however, the question had become obsolete. It was not a matter of distinguishing between those who were and those who were not one's neighbor. It was a matter of being a neighbor to others.

In the Old Testament the law of love was restricted to one's neighbor, one's fellow Israelites, and to resident aliens. Jesus extended it to include one's enemies and even one's persecutors. Loving one's enemies is considered one of the unique aspects of the ethics of Jesus and the New Testament.

The clearest expression of the new ethic is found in Matthew 5:43-48 (see also Luke 6:27-36):

> You have heard that it was said, "You shall love your neighbor and hate your enemy." But I say to you, love your enemies, and pray for those who persecute you, that you may be children of your heavenly Father, for he makes his sun rise on the bad and the good, and causes rain to fall on the just and the unjust. For if you love those who love you, what recompense will you have? Do not the tax collectors do the same? And if you greet your brothers only, what is unusual about that? Do not the pagans do the same? So be perfect, just as your heavenly Father is perfect.

There is no commandment to hate one's enemy in the Old Testament, but the fact that the commandment not to hate was restricted to one's neighbor, that is to one who belonged to God's chosen people, and to the resident alien led many to assume that there was such a commandment or that the existing commandment could be interpreted that way, as can be inferred from Matthew 5:43.

By extending the law of love to include our enemies and even those who persecute us, Jesus meant to include all human beings. In Jesus' teaching, this universality is based on the view of God as Creator and Sustainer of all. The new ethic of love flows from the event of creation and has its source in God as Creator. It consequently overflows the boundaries set for the ethic of love in the Israelite covenant, which flowed from Israel's liberation and had its source in God as the Lord of the Israelite covenant. Hence the need for a new covenant which would be open and offered to all human beings and would invite the whole human race to join in one people of God.

The new covenant is not just a second covenant. It is radically new, and its newness is first reflected in its universality. The new covenant, in its divine source, in principle and in vision, if not in historical realization, is coextensive with God's sovereign role as Creator and with the reign of God.

Worship in the new covenant is also radically new, as is the ethical response for which it calls. But what is it that makes these radically new? Why do we speak at all of a new covenant and a new commandment? The issue is one of Christology.

At the heart of the new covenant and its set of relationships is the person of Jesus Christ who is Lord of all. The central act of worship in the covenant is the Lord's Supper, whose meaning flows from the great Christ-event, the passion-resurrection, and Jesus' abiding state as risen Lord. It is from Jesus' title as Lord that we grasp the extraordinary scope of the ethical responsibility demanded by the Lord's Supper. It is from Jesus' title as Christ that we grasp the extraordinary depth of commitment demanded by the Lord's Supper.

The Greek expression for "the Lord's Supper" is *to kuriakon deipnon*, which appears only once in the New Testament but in a very important text on the Christian assembly at Corinth. I have already cited that text: "When you meet in one place, then, it is not to eat the Lord's Supper" (1 Cor 11:20).

Note that the word *kuriakon* is an adjective and not a noun. There is no equivalent for that adjective in English. As a result, we tend to think of the Lord's Supper as the supper of the Lord, *to deipnon tou kuriou,* which would indicate a meal that was offered by or presided over by the Lord. That is the meaning of the expression, "the table of the Lord," where "Lord" (*kurios*) is a noun. The expression *to kuriakon deipnon* presupposes that the Lord offers and presides over the supper but it goes further and describes a meal that draws its meaning from the Lord and is inspired by the Lord.

To appreciate the ethical implications of the Lord's Supper, the Christian meal of the new covenant, we must inquire into the meaning and implications of Jesus' title as Lord. For this I call attention to three texts, one of which refers to Jesus as "our Lord," another to Jesus as "Lord," and the third to Jesus as "Lord of all."

The first text, Romans 1:3-4, distinguishes Jesus' historical existence as a Jew, "descended from David according to the flesh," from his risen state:

> . . . the gospel about his Son, descended from David according to the flesh, but established as Son of God in power according to the spirit of holiness through resurrection from the dead, Jesus Christ our Lord.

The origins of this text lie very likely in a creed, a profession of faith. Hence its reference to "our Lord." The newly baptized, for example, would be expected to apply Jesus' universal lordship to themselves personally by calling him "our Lord." The Lord of all was their Lord, not only as individuals but as belonging to the people of God. Hence the plural personal pronoun, "our."

The second text, Philippians 2:9-11, speaks of Jesus' exaltation above all personal beings save the Father. It forms part of an early Christological hymn (Phil 2:6-11) calling on all creation, in the heavens, on the earth, and below the earth, to bend the knee at the name of Jesus. The hymn concludes with an expression of urgency that "every tongue confess that Jesus Christ is Lord, to the glory of God the Father." The hymn presupposes that those who sing it acknowledge Jesus Christ as their Lord and invites them to unite with all of creation in confessing Jesus' universal lordship. Jesus is not only their Lord, but the Lord of all creation. Therefore, they turn to him not only as members of the people of God but as part of all creation.

The third text is from Peter's discourse in the home of the Gentile Cornelius:

> In truth, I see that God shows no partiality. Rather, in every nation whoever fears him and acts uprightly is acceptable to him. You know the word that he sent to the Israelites as he proclaimed peace through Jesus Christ, who is Lord of all (Acts 10:34-36).

Jesus is not just our Lord. He is the Lord of all, including those who have not yet committed themselves to the new covenant. The text goes on to indicate that those who ate and drank with Jesus after he rose from the dead, that is those who shared in the Lord's Supper, are witnesses to his entire life, including his new risen life. That is why they had to preach to all that Jesus, the risen Lord, was judge of the living and the dead. The expression "the living and the dead" includes absolutely everybody. Leaving no one out, it is as inclusive a biblical expression as one can find.

What does Peter's discourse say about the ethical responsibility of those who recognize Jesus as their Lord, as the Lord of creation, and as the Lord of all? What does it say of those who participate at the Lord's Supper, who assemble at the table of the one who is their Lord, the Lord of creation and the Lord of all? It says that by reason of their table solidarity with the one they embrace as Lord of all they have no choice but to extend their concern to all, even to those who do not recognize Jesus as their Lord and who may not even know of the Lord's Supper. For the Christian, one's neighbor includes all those for whom Jesus is Lord, and that means the entire human race.

Such is the scope of the ethical responsibility demanded by the Lord's Supper. The story of Acts dwells on the early Christian struggle to fulfill that demand even with regard to those who already had entered the new covenant. In Jerusalem, for example, the newer Greek-speaking members of the community had grounds to complain that their widows were being neglected while those of the Hebrew-speaking members were provided for (see Acts 6:1-7).

To grasp the implications of the text, which describes a situation not unlike that of 1 Corinthians 11, we need to focus for a moment on the position of widows in the ancient world. In Israelite, Jewish, Roman, and Greek law, a young girl was subject to her father. When she married, she was subject to her husband. She had no rights on her own. When her husband died, she inherited none of his wealth and property. These went to her sons, particularly the oldest. If she had no son, or her son refused to provide for her, and if her father was unable or unwilling to provide for her, she was absolutely helpless.

In early Christian writing, as in the contemporary Jewish writing, the widow thus became the personal symbol of the helpless poor. The community of those who broke bread together at the Lord's Supper therefore had a special obligation to provide for the widow. The same applies to the orphan. Without the community seeing to their needs, widows and orphans were left to the streets and easily victimized.

The issue of ethical responsibility can be summed up in terms of inclusiveness and exclusiveness. For whom are we responsible? Is it only for those who join us for worship? Is the invitation to join in worship addressed to all? Is anyone excluded? The importance of the inclusive-exclusive polarity can be appreciated by reviewing all the meals with Jesus in Luke's Gospel, beginning with those taken with the risen Lord and working backwards through the life of Jesus. We see it, for example, in the way Jesus responds to the Pharisees who ask why Jesus' disciples eat and drink with tax collectors and sinners (Luke 5:27-32; see 15:1-32) and in the way he defends the presence of a woman who was regarded as a sinner when she came to him while he was dining in the home of a Pharisee (Luke 7:36-50). Jesus always comes down on the side of inclusiveness, and he confronts those, notably the Pharisees, who insist on excluding others from the meal. In these meals, Jesus is present as a prophetic figure anticipating the demands of the Lord's Supper and the breaking of the bread in the reign of God (see Luke 14:15).

The Lord's Supper makes demands concerning the scope of a Christian's ethical commitment. It also makes demands with regard to its depth. It is not just a matter of extending one's concern to all. It is also a matter of committing one's whole being to all. This can best be seen from the example of Jesus' commitment at the Last Supper, where he showed willingness to lay down his life.

The New Testament never allows the Lord's Supper to be separated from the Last Supper. The Eucharist is at once the Lord's Supper and the memorial of the passion and death of Christ. Even

Paul, in the passage which gives us the name "the Lord's Supper," tells the Corinthians that whenever they eat that bread and drink that cup—that is, whenever they partake of the bread and the cup of the Lord's Supper—they proclaim the death of the Lord until he comes (1 Cor 11:26).

The intimate relationship of the Lord's Supper and the memorial of the passion-resurrection of Christ is also plain from the stories of the breaking of bread at the end of Luke's Gospel (24:13-35, 36-49). The disciples were unable even to recognize the risen Lord, let alone follow through on their mission, without coming to terms with the passion and death of Jesus. The reason is clear. Those who joined Jesus in the Lord's Supper had to die to all that prevented them from assuming ethical responsibility for all human beings.

So it is that the Gospels present the great liturgical texts of the Lord's Supper in the context of Jesus' Last Supper. In that context, the participants are asked to do what Jesus did and to do this in memory of him. They are asked to take on his attitude and offer their lives that others might truly live.

The Lord's Supper texts are the liturgical expression of those earlier parts of the Gospel which depict the following of Christ as a taking up of one's cross. Separated from the memorial of the Christ event, the Lord's Supper is not a vision but a mirage. Joined to the memorial, it reveals the depth of commitment required to make the vision of the Lord's Supper a reality.

Conclusion

The Bible is very clear on the ethical responsibility demanded by worship, in both the Old and New Testaments. It is also clear regarding the difficulty of fulfilling those demands. But it never backs down from them. Its storytellers and prophets do not allow their hearers and readers to forget that what is at stake is the value of their worship. Apart from ethical responsibility, their worship becomes worthless.

It took nearly the whole of biblical history to recognize that the entire human race was our neighbor. That recognition came through successive manifestations of grace in the long biblical journey. There was the Mosaic covenant and the formation of a special people of God, when the neighbor included only those who belonged to that people. This covenant had special concern for the alien residing among the people of God. Then there was the new covenant in the blood and life of Christ the Lord. The neighbor now included all human beings. Jesus Christ is not only our Lord. He is the Lord of all.

The Lord's Supper represented a tremendous challenge for the early Christian community. The New Testament provides clear witness to their failures in living up to that challenge. The Lord's Supper remains a tremendous challenge for us, as well, in that it contains the essential agenda for our Christian life and mission.

3
Preaching Social Justice: The Lectionary and the Persian Gulf War

William Skudlarek, O.S.B.

Liturgical preaching on social justice is a necessary consequence of the fact that the Bible is a constituent element of liturgical celebration. The Scriptures we read and proclaim in the Christian assembly bring us into the presence of a God who witnesses the affliction of the descendants of Abraham, hears their cry of complaint, and comes down to rescue them (see Exod 3:7-8). According to Luke's Gospel, Jesus inaugurates his ministry at the synagogue in Nazareth by quoting a text of the Prophet Isaiah to announce that he has come

> to bring glad tidings to the poor,
> to proclaim liberty to captives,
> recovery of sight to the blind
> and release to prisoners,
> to announce a year of favor from the Lord (Luke 4:18b-19).

The God revealed in the Scriptures is a God whose passion for justice knows no time or season. However, while the subject of social justice cannot be absent from liturgical preaching, one could certainly argue that it need not always be in the forefront or explicitly developed. The Bible also speaks of a God who is found in the depths of the human heart, nearer to us than we are to ourselves, as Augustine would say. But there are moments when particular issues of social justice present themselves with such urgency that they simply must be addressed. The war in the Persian Gulf was surely one of the those moments.

Participants in the focus session on preaching social justice were asked to recall and describe the preaching they had heard on the feast of the Baptism of the Lord and on the Second Sunday in Ordinary Time. The dates for these two Sundays were January 12 and 19, 1991, the Sundays immediately before and after the January 15 deadline that our President had set for Iraq to withdraw from Kuwait.

One person remembered that the pastor (very good preacher) in her cathedral parish said nothing at all about the situation in the Persian Gulf on the Sunday before January 15. Instead, he announced a prayer service for the evening of January 14. When she expressed her disappointment, saying that while a special prayer service was important and good, the issue needed to be addressed above all in the Sunday assembly, he answered that he did not feel he was able to speak about it at the Sunday Eucharist, because whatever he may have said there would have been too divisive.

Another person described the powerful homily a permanent deacon had preached in her parish. He was a retired Air Force officer, who had been stationed in the Persian Gulf for many years. He recounted how close he and his family had become to the people during their years in that part of the world, and how much they had come to admire both the human and religious qualities of Arab Muslims. Now his son was serving in the Air Force and had been posted to the Persian Gulf region. He concluded his homily by asking, "And now what am I to think, as my own son is over there, preparing to drop bombs on a people I have come to admire and love?"

A minister recounted his own anguish as a preacher, feeling he had to speak against the war in order to be faithful to the Gospel, but sensing that his words were causing resistance more than they were bringing about a change of heart and mind.

Another spoke of how the staff of a parish located near a military base struggled with what should and should not be said in the Sunday homily as the United States approached the brink of war. They finally agreed that the issue could not be avoided or soft pedaled, and that the homilist should try to explain why the parish ministers believed going to war was not an appropriate response to the situation in the Persian Gulf. Expecting outcries of indignation from the members of the parish who were connected with the military, they instead received more thanks than objections from these same parishioners who said, "Thank God there is at least one place where we can talk and think about the moral implications of what we are about."

After the participants had had a chance to speak about what they heard in the sermons and homilies that were given on those two Sundays, we turned to the texts that the Roman Catholic Lectionary appointed to be read on the feast of the Baptism of the Lord (January 12, 1991) and on the Second Sunday in Ordinary Time in year B (January 19, 1991). Of those who recalled a homily or sermon that dealt with the issue of the war on those two Sundays, no one was able to remember a single reference to the scriptural texts from the Lectionary. Several, however, did remember homilies on January 12 which spoke about the baptism of Christ but made no mention whatsoever of the situation in the Persian Gulf.

On January 12 the first lesson was from Isaiah 42. It began:

> Here is my servant whom I uphold,
> my chosen one with whom I am pleased,
> Upon whom I have put my spirit;
> he shall bring forth justice to the nations,
> Not crying out, not shouting,
> not making his voice heard in the street.
> A bruised reed he shall not break,
> and a smoldering wick he shall not quench,
> Until he establishes justice on the earth;
> the coastlands will wait for his teaching (Isa 42:1-4).

Even if a preacher were to hesitate about identifying Iraq as a bruised reed or a smoldering wick, it is hard to avoid the conclusion that the servant whom God sends to establish justice on the earth is one who does not resort to violence to accomplish his mission.

The responsorial psalm put the following refrain in the mouths of the congregation: "The Lord will bless his people with peace" (Ps 29:11).

The second lesson was taken from the discourse which Peter gave in the house of Cornelius as recounted in chapter 10 of the Acts of the Apostles. The message God sent to the children of Israel, Peter announces, is "the good news of peace" proclaimed through Jesus Christ who is the Lord of all.

Finally, the Gospel from the first chapter of Mark spoke of the baptism of Jesus by John, after which the sky is rent in two and the Spirit descends on him like a dove.

After only a brief perusal of these texts it quickly became apparent how suited they were to shape a homily that could, at the very least, raise serious questions about war as an appropriate way to establish justice and peace, especially for those who are baptized into the body of Christ and who therefore share in the messianic mission given him in his baptism. But of the approximately sixty people from all parts of the country who attended this focus session, not one was able to remember a single homily that drew on these texts to address the fact that within the week this country would resort to violence to combat injustice and protect its economic and strategic interests.

How does one explain this glaring disregard for such appropriate scriptural texts? My guess is that preachers simply presumed that since January 12 was a major feast, and since the Lectionary texts had been chosen to correspond to that feast, there was clearly no possibility that they would be able to speak to the then current concern about the imminent outbreak of war. In other words, there were basically two groups of preachers who set out to prepare their homilies during the week before January 12: First, there were those who said, "I simply have to preach about war this Sunday," and who did not bother to look at the Lectionary on the presumption that it would not have anything to offer. And second, there were those who said, for whatever reason, "I cannot preach about war this Sunday," and who, if they used the Lectionary, were unable or unwilling to hear how powerfully those texts spoke of God's servant, anointed and sent to bring forth justice to the nations, to announce a year of favor from the Lord.

One of the keys to effective liturgical preaching on issues of social justice is to allow questions of poverty, violence, war, or human rights to become one of the partners in dialogue with the Scriptures that the preacher gives voice to in the midst of the assembly.

In a liturgical tradition such as ours, the Scriptural texts to be read at the Sunday celebration are determined before-hand. They are a given. But to those texts the preacher must bring the issues, concerns, and questions of the congregation that gathers for worship in order to find in those texts a "word from the Lord." At times—and perhaps far too often in an individualistic and narcissistic society such as ours—those issues and concerns will be deeply personal in nature: How can I feel good about myself? How can I forgive someone who has hurt me? Why does God seem so absent from my life? But if the preacher is willing to bring broader social concerns and questions to the Scriptures, congregations may be able to rediscover that the Word of God is a word that calls us to fashion and be citizens of a new world order built on justice and love, a word that points to righteousness as the fruit of faith and the sign of God's presence.

We then turned briefly to the texts which the Roman Lectionary appoints to be read on the Second Sunday of Ordinary Time (year B), which in 1991 fell on January 19, the Sunday following the outbreak of violence in the Persian Gulf.

What first attracted my attention when I consulted these texts was the citation for the first lesson: 1 Samuel 3:3b-10, 19. Obviously something had been left out. The pericope describes God's threefold call to the boy Samuel as he lay sleeping in the temple. The text, as it appears in the Lectionary, ends as follows:

> When Samuel went to sleep in his place, the Lord came and revealed his presence, calling out as before, "Samuel, Samuel!" Samuel answered, "Speak, for your servant is listening." Samuel grew up, and the Lord was with him, not permitting any word of his to be without effect (1 Sam 3:9b-10, 19).

In its Lectionary form, the text gives the impression that God did not say anything to Samuel, in spite of Samuel's plea to God to speak, and his declaration that he was ready to listen. However, when we turn to the Bible, this is what we find:

> When Samuel went to sleep in his place, the Lord came and revealed his presence, calling out as before, "Samuel, Samuel!" Samuel answered, "Speak, for your servant is listening." The Lord said to Samuel: "I am about to do something in Israel that will cause the ears of everyone who hears it to ring. On that day

I will carry out in full against Eli everything I threatened against his family. I announce to him that I am condemning his family once and for all, because of this crime: though he knew his sons were blaspheming God, he did not reprove them. Therefore, I swear to the family of Eli that no sacrifice or offering will ever expiate its crime." Samuel then slept until morning, when he got up early and opened the doors of the temple of the Lord. He feared to tell Eli the vision, but Eli called to him, "Samuel, my son!" He replied, "Here I am." Then Eli asked, "What did he say to you? Hide nothing from me! May God do thus and so to you if you hide a single thing he told you." So Samuel told him everything, and held nothing back. Eli answered, "He is the Lord. He will do what he judges best" (1 Sam 3:11-18).

Once again, no one remembered a homily which addressed the war—which was now in full progress in the Persian Gulf—that drew on or made use of the Scriptural texts for this Sunday. Furthermore, no one present at this session who was involved in the ministry of preaching had gone to the Bible to check on the verses that had been left out of the text of the Sunday's first reading.

What we can learn from this particular example is that preachers need to bring a healthy "ideological suspicion" to their reading of liturgical pericopes and, at times, to the Scriptures themselves. We need to ask, for example, what (or who) is being left out, and why. Whose interests are being protected? Whose voice is not being heard?

As we saw in examining the texts for the Baptism of the Lord, preaching on issues of social justice demands a profound respect for the Scriptures, a willingness to listen to them, a readiness to believe that the pericopes appointed to be read on a particular day for no other reason than that they follow a sequential reading of a biblical book or that they correspond to the theme of a feast or season, may very well be able to address a saving word to the issues and concerns of contemporary society.

But, having said this, it is important to be aware of the fact that scriptural texts also reflect the limited perspectives of their human authors, and further, that the choice of liturgical readings can reveal the interests or even prejudices of the compilers of the Lectionary as much as the intentionality of the word of God.

The question, then, is why were 1 Samuel 3:11-18 omitted from the first lesson? In the *Introduction to the Lectionary,* under the section devoted to "Criteria for the Choice and Arrangement of Readings," an explanation is offered for the dropping of certain verses from Lectionary readings:

> d) *Omission of verses:* Many liturgies, including the Roman liturgy, traditionally omit certain verses from biblical readings. One should not be too quick to do this because the style, purpose, or meaning of the scriptural text may easily be damaged. But, for pastoral reasons, it seemed best to continue this tradition, taking care that the essential meaning of the text remain unchanged. Otherwise some texts would be too lengthy or readings of greater spiritual value to the people would have to be entirely omitted because of the one or two verses of little pastoral worth or involving truly difficult questions (*Introduction to the Lectionary,* No 7).

While one may agree with this rationale in general, its application to this particular text from 1 Samuel raises some serious questions. Are the omitted verses judged to be "of little pastoral worth" or do they involve "truly difficult questions" simply because the word which God speaks to Samuel is a word of condemnation? Is this to imply that when we come to hear the word of God, we will only listen if the word spoken is a word that confirms our position, our understanding of what is right and good?

Would it not, especially on this Sunday, have been salutary, in the fullest sense of the word, to have heard the Lord uttering a word of condemnation against a priest who knew his sons were blaspheming God but did not correct them? This text might have provided preachers with a way of helping congregations resistant to any intrusion of "politics" in the pulpit understand that it is precisely because they are priests ministering to a priestly people that they have the duty, often a painful one, of preaching a word which questions, challenges, and corrects peoples' thoughts and actions. In this way, the assembly, with heart and mind renewed, may offer God a pure sacrifice of praise and thanksgiving.

A healthy "ideological suspicion" of the lectionary text for the first lesson on the Sunday after the outbreak of war in the Persian Gulf might have afforded preachers an opportunity to engage the congregation in a dialogue with the Scriptures on a matter of profound concern to everyone. It might have helped to give the Christian community a way of understanding what was happening in the Persian Gulf that would have been far different from the chauvinistic interpretation provided by the White House and the Pentagon and uncritically broadcast by the media.

We can thus see that liturgical preachers have to bring to the Scriptures, and especially to Lectionary pericopes, both the simplicity of doves and the wisdom of serpents. Trusting in the power of God's Word, preachers will go to the Lectionary with the confidence that even though the pericopes were not chosen with our particular situation in mind, they may very well be able to become partners in a dialogue with our predicament and speak a saving word to it.

On the other hand, recognizing that the Word of God comes to us through human authors and human editors, preachers must also be attentive to the ways these authors and editors may have shaped that word to serve their own purposes, even omitting portions which they judged to be problematic or of no value. At times it will be by attending to these silenced voices that preachers will be able to hear and proclaim the Word that God wishes to speak to the world today.

4

Liturgy and Social Consciousness

R. Kevin Seasoltz, O.S.B.

In a book published in 1979, Phillip Hallie tells a true story of deeply religious people who were profoundly formed by the Word of God, people who opened their lives Sunday after Sunday to the wisdom and strength of God's Word and then as prophetic people living in obedience to God's Word shared their lives and possessions with others, above all with those in dire need.

The story is called *Lest Innocent Blood Be Shed*.[1] It opens with a knock on the door of a Protestant Huguenot parsonage in Vichy, France, during the Second World War one night during a raging snowstorm. As later recalled by the Jewish fugitive who stood shuddering on the doorstep, Magda Trocmé, the pastor's wife, opened the door, looked at the stranger asking for entry and cried, "Come in, come in," as she drew the Jewish woman into the warmth of her kitchen. The pastor's wife was as aware as everyone else in the village of Le Chambon of the penalty for harboring Jews—death for both the Jews and those who harbored them. Yet the refugee who stepped across her threshold that bitter night was only the first of hundreds who were given shelter, fed, and escorted to freedom from the farmhouses, schools and barns of Le Chambon. Years afterwards when asked what had made them risk their lives for unknown Jews, the people of Le Chambon found the question disconcerting. One after another they hesitated, and after a few moments of silence they replied, "We had no choice. They would have died without us." As they had all shared in the table fellowship of worship year after year, so they all shared Magda Trocmé's immediate, characteristic response, "Come in, come in." In the Jews on their threshold they implicitly would have recognized the life of Christ that was at the center of their common worship, a life that they shared week after week through the Word of God in Jesus Christ and the embrace of the Holy Spirit. "Truly I tell you, just as you did it to one of the least of those who are members of my family, you did it to me" (Matt 25:40).

The story raises hard questions for all Christians who by initiation are committed to laying down their lives for others just as Jesus Christ laid down his life for us. It raises critical questions for all who are presumably formed by the Word of God week after week, year after year, and who are through baptism publicly committed to bear prophetic witness to the meaning and ethical implications of Christ's death and resurrection and the outpouring of the Holy Spirit on all of creation. What difference, then, does the celebration of Christ's paschal mystery make in the way Christians live and relate to God, to the world and to one another?

Trinitarian Character of Liturgy

Christian liturgy is primarily the celebration of the work of God in Jesus Christ acting through the power of the Holy Spirit.[2] It is that Trinitarian work which is given expression in assemblies of believers who face contemporary ethical and political issues and therefore turn to God in Jesus Christ through the power of the Holy Spirit, present and operative in human hearts and communities. Christians turn to God in order to appropriate the gift of their saving history and to express and deepen their faith and their communion with God and each other.[3] As a result they have a distinctive identity which is expressed and hopefully strengthened through liturgical celebration. This sense of identity empowers them to live and relate to themselves, to others, and to the world as God lives and relates to all of creation in Jesus Christ through the Holy Spirit. Christian liturgy has a Trinitarian shape. It expresses the inner life of God revealed in Jesus Christ as three persons in one God, as both personal and communal. God's own consciousness revealed in Jesus Christ is both personal and social.[4]

The liturgy also expresses the self-gift of the incarnate Son of God offered to the Father through the power of the Holy Spirit, a self-gift offered also to God's people. His was a life spent for God and others but one which ended in his own death on the cross.[5] He was put to death by people who were threatened by his commitment to God and God's people. But Jesus was rewarded by his Father who raised him from the dead so he could be for us the source of God's own Holy Spirit, a Spirit empowering us to lay down our lives for God and for one another.[6] Hence Jesus Christ not only reveals the face of God; he also reveals the face of humanity made in the image and likeness of God. Humanity then is both personal and communal. It follows that the whole of Christian life is meant to have a Trinitarian character.[7]

The Covenant

God's relationship with the people of the world was first formalized by the covenant.[8] For Israel this was primarily the Mosaic covenant which was regularly renewed in a liturgical context. The celebration of God's saving deeds by formally remembering them was an obvious way of praising God and of committing the assembly of believers once again to respond to the gift of the covenant as God's faithful people.[9] The covenant was both a gift and a demand for a response—that the people live as God's people should live. The way of life expected of God's people was summarized in the Decalogue. Hence, both liturgy and life were meant to be expressions of fidelity to the covenant.[10]

This is no less true of the new covenant made in Jesus Christ. But for the new Israel—for us—liturgical celebrations are not simply the context in which worshipers recall God's great deeds in Jesus Christ. Christian liturgy makes the person of Jesus Christ present in Word and sacrament so that worshiping communities not only have an effective model of how they should live set before them; they also are offered an effective power, the gift of Jesus Christ's own Holy Spirit, which enables them to live and act in the manner of the Lord Jesus.[11] Christian life is a covenanted life in which one is initiated into the very life of God through baptism, confirmation, and Holy Eucharist and so bonded to God by the gift of the Holy Spirit that one is enabled to live and act as Jesus Christ would live and act.

Passover and Exodus

Closely related to the covenant aspect of both liturgy and life are the themes of passover and exodus. These themes were prominent in the lives of the Israelites; consequently, they were strongly reflected in the liturgical celebrations of the First Covenant and are emphasized in the liturgies of Jewish communities today.[12] But the Passover and the Exodus also have a distinctive meaning in the life of Jesus Christ and the celebration of Christian liturgy by his disciples.[13] Jesus passed over from death to life; he rejected the false idols of power and pleasure, while committing himself to the Father as the ultimate source of meaning and value in his life. He entered deeply into the healing and corrective dimensions of life and brought light where there was darkness and life where there was death. Just as he himself died to the temptation to isolation, self-preoccupation and self-sufficiency, so he invited and empowered others to take up their cross daily by responsibly embracing the gift of the Holy Spirit, the Spirit of the all-living God who comes to us moment by moment in the context of other living people.[14]

In baptism Christians die with Christ and rise to new life. In the Eucharist they acknowledge their total dependence on Christ and share again in his experience of dying and rising. Thus they are nourished by the Word of God and the living Bread and saving Cup so they might live in the world with the same willingness to struggle for human rights and responsibilities. The response of Christian living knows no other way than the way of the Lord Jesus. Jesus himself had to pass from his baptismal experience of unconditional acceptance—"You are my beloved Son; in you I take delight" (Mark 1:11)—to the desert experience of loneliness and trial. He had to come to grips with the mystery of life, tap his own hidden inner resources, confront the iniquity rampant in life, and above all confirm the ultimacy of God. The way of suffering, the way of the cross, was the way to liberation, to freedom, and to eternal life. So it must be in the lives of all of us who profess to be disciples of the Lord Jesus. Intimate human relations with God and other human persons are frequently spoiled by an inability to understand and accept the positive role of suffering. It is often experienced as failure, but in fact it can be the ground for personal and communal growth. And, of course, growth at any age is painful.[15]

In one of his plays, Eugene O'Neill wrote that "Man is born broken, he lives by mending; the grace of God is glue."[16] In our better moments we know that the brokenness and the burdens of life are not pointless. But it is sometimes difficult to go on convincing ourselves. When a person we love suddenly dies or has a violent accident, when a little child develops cancer, when an important relationship is frustrated, when we see people hungry, poorly housed, and inadequately clothed, depression and perhaps despair may set in. We might feel marooned in pain.[17] But in the course of time it often happens that many mysterious events seem to work together for good. Life is something we live forward but understand only backward. We come to grasp the positive meaning and value of what at one time appeared to be madness.

Christian initiation, as the celebration in which the community affirms life on its deepest levels, is meant to move Christians into the life and mission of Christ himself. It is most fundamentally a call to life, to love, to communion of life with God and all of God's people. Yet before we are asked to love others, we are first of all loved by the Spirit of God operating through the community which symbolizes God's love for all people in Christ and through the power of the Holy Spirit. In other words, the baptismal experience of Christ himself is meant to be our experience through the communication of his Spirit in and through our baptismal liturgy.[18] The contemporary quality of Christ's baptismal experience was captured imaginatively by the British painter Stanley Spencer in his scenes from the gospels which were set in his native village of Cookham.[19] In the painting *Baptism by John,* Jesus is immersed in the River Thames at Cookham, with people in bathing suits all around him. He would probably have agreed that a Christ who is not contemporary and who does not live with us in our time through the power of the Holy Spirit is not really the Christ.

The Lord Jesus invites us who are sometimes, perhaps often weary and burdened to come to him. He does not promise that he will take away our burdens, but he does guarantee us refreshment and peace. The New Testament regularly protests against a spirituality without suffering and conflict; it protests against the false illusion that God is to be found apart from Jesus Christ crucified. If we want to be reformed in God's image and share in the risen life of Christ, we must first of all be in the image of Jesus on the cross.[20] However the acceptance of suffering must not be equated with passivity, indifference or abstract endurance. Such responses in fact harden the human heart and dehumanize the person. The real self never surfaces. The trap that is set for us was exemplified in an amusing but disturbing Charles Addams cartoon in *The New Yorker:* two women are looking at an enormous blob sitting in an armchair. The only signs of life are its beady eyes. One woman turns to the other and says: "We're still waiting for Stanley to jell."[21] Sometimes we are tempted to yield up all responsibility, all initiative, all choice. We refuse the gift of God's Spirit and become "blobs" that never jell. In fact we are called to confront suffering and struggle through it so we may become more capable of love—and more capable of suffering. In bearing our cross, our isolation and our self-protection are often broken open so that in our hearts there is more room for others, above all for God.

The prophecy of Isaiah proclaims that the way of the just will be smooth with rich food and choice wines for all along the way.[22] But most of us, I am sure, know of those who have tried to walk the way of justice and peace whose faces are worn and whose bodies are weary. The powerful picture of Dorothy Day in the *National Catholic Reporter* a number of years ago comes to mind. She is sitting on a stool in a Chavez boycott line, her face to the hot California sun, her wrinkled hands grasping her knees. Persons who are especially sensitive to the ways of God, to the dreams for the world that were entertained by the prophets and above all by Jesus—those people often experience a pain that is not shared by others, a pain of weariness and sadness that frequently shows on their faces.[23] This was expressed by Galway Kinnell when he wrote:

> What storms have blown me, and from where,
> What dreams have drowned, or half-dead, here
> Surround me, or whether I am old or young,
> I cannot find an answer on my tongue.
> Yet if you ask me to describe that dark, wild
> Winter of the eyes, then I
> Can speak, answer endlessly,
> For that look was not on me as a child.
> Each year I lived I watched the fissure
> Between what was and what I wished for
> Widen, until there was nothing left

> But the gulf of emptiness.
> Most men have not seen the world divide,
> Or seen, it did not open wide,
> Or wide, they clung to the safer side.
> But I have felt the sundering like a blade.[24]

Is the way of justice and love always smooth? Certainly the image of the reign of God as a banquet is often tried and tested, purified even, when we see hatred and injustice living side by side with those who celebrate liturgy every Sunday and claim to be disciples of Jesus Christ. Perceptive people grow disillusioned by institutional violence and benign indifference. At that moment one must be just with one's own consciousness and one's own conscience. It is then that one learns the meaning of honesty and truth, that one learns how to respond to the presence of God's Spirit in the human heart calling for a deeper entry into the paschal mystery of Jesus Christ in order to share in the transformation of the world. The meaning of the banquet is transposed to a level where hope for the future becomes the great source of nourishment that one offers to others.

Christian Ethical Life in Community

The exodus accomplished in Jesus is to some extent shared with Christians in baptism, but baptism launches Christians on a journey which must last all life long.[25] We spend our whole lives becoming the Christians we are called to be. Although we have died together with Jesus and have risen with him to a new life, we are still en route to where Jesus sits in glory. The path we have to follow always takes us through the world. As we live in the world we do not know precisely where fidelity to Jesus Christ will lead us. We do know that along the way we will be supported by the presence of the Spirit of God. We will be nourished by the Eucharist, but the specific contours of our journey remain in many ways unknown to us. We journey by faith not by full knowledge; consequently major decisions have to be made along the way.[26]

Christian life has often been stymied by a failure to recognize that one is called to venture into the unknown future. The strong faith of Abraham has often been replaced by a calculating shrewdness which prefers a clear blueprint to an uncharted course. But such an attitude excludes almost any genuine decision-making and the risks decisions always involve. God's invitation to us in Christ is not something that we initiate, nor can the risks involved in Christian living be eliminated by human calculation. In the liturgy the ground over which one must journey is set out symbolically and food for the journey is shared; the ground, however, is often unfamiliar and the terrain rugged and steep. The symbols are always ambiguous; they yield their meaning only to those who are willing to engage in the task of interpretation. The interpretation is a prelude to judgments and decisions about one's life.

Our English word "decision" comes from the Latin *decidere,* and implies an amputation, a cutting off of something, a choice of certain possibilities and an elimination of others. "If your hand or your foot causes your downfall, cut it off and fling it away; it is better for you to enter into life maimed or lame, than to keep two hands or two feet and be thrown into the eternal fire" (Matt 18:8). What is the hand or foot that Jesus speaks of in the Gospel? Is it the color of our skin, our gender, our wealth, our religion, or our ethnic background? What is it that shackles us with a false sense of security and keeps us from moving into a redeeming future?

Institutionalized religious bodies have always been in danger of introversion, of encapsulating the Spirit of God, of masquerading as God in the midst of the world. In this regard one might think of Federico Fellini's film *8 1/2* in which Guido, who is anguished by the emptiness of his life, in desperation arranges to meet the cardinal at the baths. Ensconced in steam but wearing his buckled shoes and his scarlet zuchetto, the cardinal has a smug and facile answer to Guido's plight as he responds in the solemn tones of a sacred oracle: *Extra ecclesiam nulla salus.* "Outside the Church there is no salvation." The cardinal is like Joshua in the Bible who wanted to confine the Spirit of the Lord to the seventy elders and complained that others were prophesying in the camp. And Moses asks the hard question, "Are you jealous? Would that all the people of the Lord were prophets. Would that the Lord might bestow his Spirit on them all" (Num 11:29).

Whatever the evidence, the future belongs to those who embrace it. It belongs to those who seek the truth and remain confident of the power of the powerless, the gentle, the repentant, and the poor; confident of the power of simplicity which scorns rich idols; confident of the power of those who are voices of the voiceless; confident of the power of those who stand by the intrinsic value of the truth and goodness implanted in their lives and their communities by the power of God's Spirit.

Liturgy as Disclosure Model

The liturgy provides us with an important disclosure model for sharing those meanings which we now hold and for searching for new meanings as we move into the future. It is in the liturgy that we celebrate the death, resurrection, and full life of Jesus Christ; it is there in a special way that we open our lives to the gift of the Holy Spirit. The Spirit of the Lord Jesus is with us now, but in another sense the Lord Jesus is out in front of us calling us along the path of transformation here and now so we might become fully transformed in the future. Ours is not a dormitory Church. We are meant to spend our days actively engaged in life. In imitation of Jesus Christ and through the power of the Holy Spirit we are meant to respond to a call to ongoing conversion away from sin and death to God and the fullness of life. To live in Christian faith is really to deliver oneself into the hands of God in a spirit of trust and hope. It means accepting in simplicity and openness the proclamation of the Christian story that God has raised up Jesus as Lord of all life, Lord of all creation, and that we are invited to embrace the same gift enabling us also to rise from the dead. God affirms that we are all possible.

To live in simple faith and trust appears to be easy for some people, but for most of us the ongoing decision to live by faith is the most difficult choice of all, for it means that we must live in the midst of much doubt. We doubt for many reasons, but there are decisive moments in our lives when we doubt because we are convinced that there is more to life than we are really living. If we are to grow and be transformed, we must be willing to move in new directions, explore new paths, gain deeper insights, and expand the horizons of our lives. We must be willing to go beyond what is known and familiar to what is sometimes threatening and insecure. Such doubt is costly but the transformation is worth the price.

To refuse to move into the future by accepting the creative gift of new life means that one becomes a prisoner of the present or the past. In a sense growth in faith implies loss, but it is loss for the sake of greater gain. This is the point made by the Japanese poet Masahide in a haiku he wrote:

> Since my house burned down
> I now have a better view
>   Of the rising moon.[27]

God is no spectator at life. If at times we experience God more as absent than present, it may be only to invite us to cut off and leave behind what is inferior and effete for what is good and gracious and grounded in truth.

Liturgy and Community Life

Our Christian life and our Christian liturgy are always community experiences. In fact authentic Christianity is essentially a community reality. Any opposition between individual and society falsifies the true relation, more accurately expressed in terms of person and community, which are correlative terms.[28] An individual becomes a person in and through engagement with a community. As Christians we are baptized into a community of faith and in that context we are called to develop as faithful persons. To be personal in the Christian sense one must be open to the community. In fact Christian living is possible only in the context of community. It can be understood adequately only in community and is directed toward the development of that community of all men and women as sons and daughters of God and brothers and sisters to one another.

The role of liturgy in the Christian community has often been misunderstood. For some the liturgy is simply an expression of Christian unity and community already achieved; for others it is primarily the means to achieve unity and community. In fact, the liturgy is expressive of unity achieved to some extent but it is meant to be constitutive of that unity on deeper and deeper levels. The liturgy does not confect a Christian community out of nothing, but it does deepen the faith life of the faith community.

Some sociologists of religion[29] and liturgical theologians[30] assert that religion and religious experience are communicated, shared and sustained primarily by symbols, myths, metaphors and rituals. Theological reflection and consequent doctrinal and creedal statements are said to be a second-level experience. In other words people are understood to act their way into thinking; they liturgize first, then theologize. In many cases that is probably true. But it is increasingly common today that people come to liturgy after they have espoused a certain set of doctrines or theology rather than come to espouse doctrine because of the way they have worshiped. As David Power has noted, "The mind defines before the heart exults."³¹ Likewise Christians who have a well defined sense of the Christian mystery and its personal and social implications often withdraw from liturgical assemblies which espouse either no awareness of social responsibilities or one that is contrary to the doctrines they think are compatible with their understanding of Christianity. They take advantage of the mobility that is available to them and the liturgical possibilities from which they are able to choose and so worship where they sense a consonance between liturgy and Christian life. These options unfortunately are usually not open to the poor and the elderly.

The phenomenon of reversionism is also in evidence today. David Power describes it at some length:

> This is not the resistance of the elderly or the middle-aged to change, their pertinacity in clinging to old forms of devotion, or their yearning to return to Latin Masses, Sunday services without Eucharist, or the old ways of marking the Sabbath. Nor is it simply the cultural resistance to women rabbis or bishops. It is rather the tendency, particularly among the young, to reclaim the ways of their ancestors that the generation of their parents or grandparents abandoned. Sometimes this actually takes the form of a change of allegiance: a Reform Jew joins a Hasidic synagogue, an Episcopalian joins the Roman Catholic Church, a Methodist embraces the Anglican way of worship, a Roman Catholic becomes a follower of Maurice Lefebre. More often it is an attempt to search out and win back what elders seem to have abandoned. For Jew and Christian alike, it is a search after numinous expressions that appear to have been beclouded by too much babbling and by a preoccupation with the human.³²

Reversionism often involves a search for transcendence in the midst of what is thought to be an obsession with the human. But the transcendence of God must not be recovered at the expense of the immanence of God. The worship of God must not be divorced from Christian living.

In the summer little children like to catch butterflies and bees and put them in jars so they can look at them closely and see how interesting they are. Then they usually let them go about their normal business of making the world a fascinating place in which to live. In a sense, a liturgical celebration is like a jar. It holds something precious so we can look at it closely, appreciate it more deeply, see how meaningful it is, and share its richness with others. But just as the insects die if they are kept in a jar too long, so also liturgical celebrations die; they become empty and ineffectual if they do not return us to the business of life.

This point was made in a different way by Boris Pasternak in *Doctor Zhivago* where he describes the Moscow encampment:

> The large duck was an unheard of luxury in those already hungry days, but there was no bread with it, and because of this its splendor was somehow pointless—it even got on one's nerves. . . . But the saddest thing of all was that their party was a kind of betrayal. You could not imagine anyone in the houses across the street eating or drinking in the same way at the same time. Beyond the windows lay silent, dark, hungry Moscow. Its shops were empty, and as for game and vodka, people had even forgotten to think about such things. And so it turned out that only a life similar to the life of those around us, merging with it without a ripple, is genuine life, and that an unshared happiness is not happiness, so that duck and vodka, when they seem to be the only ones in town, are not even duck and vodka. And this was most vexing of all.[33]

Genuine celebrations, be they liturgies or family meals and parties, must grow out of life and help people return to the business of life with deeper understanding, renewed strength, and invigorated hope. If Christian life is authentic, it does not lead us into narcissism; rather, it leads us to question and critique the fundamental values of society. Christian life is surely not an escape from the implications of the Lord's incarnation and our responsibility to get involved in the ongoing transformation of the world according to our talents and distinctive vocations. It implies deep confrontation with human alienation; its goal is to undermine illusion and falsehood and to promote the reign of God in all areas of human life.[34]

While sharing his life with his disciples, Jesus instructed them to do what he did by taking on his life and history. He commanded them to become members of his Body so they could come to fullness of life by being delivered from their sinfulness. That life he wanted them to share with others by healing wounds, delivering people from their isolation and alienation, and bringing others into communion with God and God's people. If the liturgy is expressive of God's life in the Lord Jesus and is celebrated with integrity, its celebrants, its assemblies, must be about the same sort of liberation. First of all they must acknowledge their own need to be delivered from alienation and isolation and then as suffering servants they must, like Jesus Christ, lay down their lives for others. They must not be concerned about their own success, prestige and prowess in the world, but rather, like Jesus, they must take their agenda from the poor and marginal people of the world.

In Luke's Gospel, Jesus condemns his disciples' concern for greatness as he instructs them, "Let the greatest among you become as the younger, and the leader as one who serves" (22:26). The Church as the community of the Lord's disciples in the world today cannot be committed to selfless ministry to others if it is simultaneously concerned about its own power and prestige or involved in any way with structures of injustice and oppression in the world. The implications of Jesus' teaching are brought out above all in John's Gospel where the account of Jesus washing the disciples' feet appears where we would expect to find the account of the institution of the Eucharist. There are several different interpretations of this text: the need for regular spiritual purification, the admonition to be humble, and the need to serve others.[35] It is certainly plausible to maintain that it is John's vivid way of showing the connection between the Eucharist and service, between liturgy and life.

The liturgy lays out a series of verbal and non-verbal symbols and puts us through a series of actions which shape our attitudes toward God, toward ourselves, toward one another and toward life in general. Creative liturgy is not about persons and communities creating imaginative liturgical celebrations but rather about the liturgy creating persons and communities in the image and likeness of God. Liturgical rites do not primarily express human feelings; they are meant to convey attitudes and dispositions. They are not primarily meant to express what we feel inside; rather, they are meant to put us in proper relationships with ourselves, others in the community, and God. In a sense, a liturgical celebration is like a dress rehearsal for the end time.[36] We put on Christ and act and relate to one another as Christ relates to us. But we also put forward our own selves, since we are only on the way to becoming one with Christ through the power of his Holy Spirit.

Liturgy and Ritual Knowledge

If we acknowledge that some people strive to develop a right understanding of theology and then search for liturgical celebrations which are consonant with that theology, we should also acknowledge that the celebration of the liturgy as ritual behavior is itself a way of coming to know theologically. Theodore Jennings explored this phenomenon in a useful article published in the *Journal of Religion*.[37] He distinguished three aspects of ritual knowledge: (1) It is acquired in and through the human body. "It is not so much that the mind 'embodies' itself in ritual action, but rather that the body 'minds' itself or attends through itself in ritual action."[38] (2) Ritual knowledge is gained not by mere detached observation but through action. Knowledge is acquired in and through the action itself. (3) Ritual knowledge is gained through engagement which is transformative of the actors. It is one experience to read about a dance, another experience to watch someone else dance the dance, and still another experience to dance the dance oneself. These three aspects of ritual knowledge can indeed be found in liturgical celebrations; that knowledge is clarified and deepened by the catechesis which precedes and follows the celebration.

The liturgy provides a context in which the celebrants can discover or rediscover who they are in the world and what the nature of their world actually is.[39] If the liturgy is celebrated as it should be celebrated, the celebrants are invited to experience themselves as persons relating to God, to others in the community and to the world as a whole. Social consciousness inevitably impinges on their lives. They are invited to see themselves not only as individuals who journey to God alone, struggling to save their souls, but as members of the Body of Christ, as persons belonging to the holy people of God who have already been saved by the paschal mystery of Jesus

Christ and who are invited together to appropriate that gift of salvation. Christian liturgy is always the liturgy of an assembly, a synaxis, a coming together in which all who are gathered by the Word of God seek to respond to God's initiating presence mediated into human lives through Word and sacrament, through both verbal and non-verbal symbols, and above all through human persons who are meant to be the primary symbols in all liturgical celebrations.

The world view set out in the celebration of Christian liturgies is at odds with the highly privatized view of religion and salvation that has often been espoused by Christians;[40] it certainly is at odds with a fundamentalist view of religion which often places decisive value on individual religious experience, individual profession of faith, and individual salvation.[41] This individualistic view of religion often gets reinforced in contemporary literature on spirituality where the language is narrow, autistic, and private, hence far removed from the broad, social language of both the Bible and the Christian liturgy.[41] It is often a language which simply advocates individual growth and fulfillment; it often shies away from the gospel theme of transformation through suffering and of death to oneself so that others might live.[42]

Certainly the behavioral sciences and psychology in particular have made important contributions to the development of personal and communal life, but they can reinforce the contemporary drive toward individualism and create a fascination with oneself, leaving one in the end alone with that fascinating self-preoccupation. The paradoxical wisdom of the Bible and the liturgy can be subtly displaced by the stages of psychological growth and personal faith development. The biblical and liturgical language which is both broad and deep gets corrupted into a language that is autistic and solipsistic, turned in on itself and on the group. In the end one is left with a preoccupation with one's own desires and agendas.[43]

The language of the liturgy transmits knowledge, but the language is often quite different from the language we are used to using, conveying meanings that are vastly different from the meanings we tend to live by in daily life. In other words, the liturgy has a strong teaching potential. As a ritual action it not only provides us with a specific point of view on reality, it also provides us with a pattern for changed behavior.[44] The rite provokes responses to the meanings, values and gifts that both ground the rite and are offered in the rite. There is no coercion but rather a loving call, an invitation to act and to relate according to the patterns that are prescribed in the ritual. So much of modern life is spent in competition with others because people are strongly motivated by success and consumerism. But in the liturgy there is no need to justify our existence; there is a need just to be there, to acknowledge our need for a Savior, for a loving God whom we find in Jesus Christ through the power of the Holy Spirit. There is the simple need to embrace the gift offered and to respond with thanksgiving and praise. If when we celebrate the liturgy, we call God our Father, it follows then that we should act not only like God's children but also as brothers and sisters to each other.[45] The frequent repetition of the Lord's Prayer in our liturgy not only teaches us the prayer itself; it also invites us to live according to the values it reveals.[46]

In a liturgical celebration, every celebrant is both an observer and a participant. If we live in faith, we acknowledge that we are always playing the role of a member of the Body of Christ, but we also acknowledge that we must play ourselves as we struggle to become more and more one in Christ. One asks then: Is the celebration of the Christian liturgy with its prayers, hymns, gestures, preaching, and movements an appropriate paradigm for human relationships in the world? Are the relationships expressed in liturgy worthy to be imitated by people struggling to follow Christ in the world? Is the liturgy a paradigm for living justly and peacefully?

A liturgy is contaminated if it does not serve as a paradigm for honest, just, loving relationships outside the celebration; it is valid to the extent that it does function in that way. Liturgical celebrations which do not correspond to the world view of Christ readily become corrupting agents in the lives of persons and communities. However, it must be noted that at present, as has often happened in past history, Christians are at variance with one another in their interpretation of what is deemed to be the authentic vision of Jesus Christ for a just world. This is especially evident in current discussions of the non-ordination of women in the Roman Catholic Church. Some Christians maintain that it is a grave injustice to prevent women from being ordained to the priesthood; others, including the *magisterium,* maintain that if justice is the establishment of the right order of things, then the non-ordination of women is just because it is in accord with the teaching of Jesus and the tradition of the Church.⁴⁷ This is obviously an area calling for both patience and sound scholarship so that the different opinions might have opportunity to be reconciled or dissolved.

As Jesus teaches, there is no opposition between God's love and true human love.⁴⁸ In Isaiah's terms, as a mother nurses her children with delight, so does God nurture the life of every human person. As a mother carries her young in her arms and fondles them in her lap, so God protects and supports each one of us. As a mother comforts her son, so God consoles all of us. God's love is like the best examples we have of human love; our human love is meant to be like the best examples we have of God's love for us.⁴⁹

To be a disciple of the Lord Jesus is above all to be a bearer of God's living Word; to be an apostle of the Lord Jesus is to bear that loving Word to others. But when disciples respond to the call to be apostles, they are often tempted to make the mistake of masquerading as little gods instead of being apostles of God in the world. They try to program other people's lives because they are convinced that they know God's will for others. They confuse God's will with their own wills for human success, control, and achievement. In the liturgy everything is call and invitation, never coercion and control.

A Model of Christian Discipleship and Apostleship

Gordon Cosby is surely one of the most impressive contemporary disciples and apostles of the Lord Jesus. He is the founder and pastor of the Church of the Savior in Washington, D.C, a church with a strong liturgical tradition and deep commitment to inner-city ministries. Cosby and the Church of the Savior have pioneered a model of Christian liturgical spirituality, church renewal, and service that works to balance the inward personal journey of faith with the outward journey of social consciousness and responsibility. They have learned what it is to be hearers of God's powerful Word and how to proclaim that Word effectively to others so that many Christians across the country have benefited from their witness and experience.

In an interview published in *Sojourners* several years ago,⁵⁰ Cosby emphasized that true disciples are those who bear the brand marks of Jesus in their bodies. Any authority they might have comes from intimacy with the Lord Jesus through the power and presence of God's own Spirit in their human hearts.

Cosby went on to reflect on what it means to be apostles of Jesus Christ. He agreed that creative and exciting ministries have been spawned by the Church of the Savior in the low-income Adams-Morgan neighborhood in Washington, but despite the best efforts and intentions of the ministers, the neighborhood has continued to deteriorate. In the spring of 1991 it was the scene of ethnic and racial violence. The experience has raised very painful issues of effectiveness, success and faithfulness. In the final analysis it has raised the question of what it means to share in the cross of Jesus Christ.

Cosby said that the whole business of effectiveness and success is so deeply ingrained within us that we tend to think of our efforts solely in terms of success, whereas the real Christian issue is our fidelity in listening to our call from God to connect with pain somewhere in God's world. The assumption many of us make is that we are going to be faithful; consequently God will bless our faithfulness with success. But we often find the cross precisely in the fact that all our amazing visions and plans come to nothing; our projects simply fail to succeed. We delude ourselves about our own possibilities; we fail to realize that the demonic is much tougher and much more resistant than we thought.

In the interview Cosby insisted that what is of ultimate value to Christians lies beyond our programs. It is what happens to people in the projects we try to implement that really matters—what happens on the deepest levels of their lives. However, access to those deepest levels is something we cannot humanly achieve. That is precisely where Christ himself working through the Holy Spirit must be God's apostle. It is the Spirit of Christ who has access to a person's inner life; it is the Spirit of Christ who accomplishes conversion. "Unless the Lord builds the house, in vain do its builders labor; unless the Lord watch over the city, in vain do the watchers keep vigil" (Ps 127:1). Cosby sees his social action programs simply as stage settings for the transforming action of Christ—very important stage settings but stage settings, nonetheless. He also maintains that it is much easier to give and to minister, to conceive and carry out programs, to sponsor demonstrations and allocate resources than it is to enter freely into one's own conversion process. Social programs often fail to get at the heart of the Christian message just as involvement in those programs often fails to get at the heart of conversion in our own lives. With a messiah complex, we tend to go off with a traveling bag full of plans for other people—plans for decisions we think they should make, plans for lives we think they should live, plans for relationships we think they should establish. Sometimes we even end up adding to others' suffering because of our ill-conceived understanding of what it means to be disciples and apostles of Jesus Christ.

In our liturgy we do not celebrate the failure of a dead messiah. We rather celebrate the fact that the one who identified with us in all our failures because he loved us so much is precisely the one whom God raised from the dead. In Gerard Manley Hopkins' lovely lines, then, we want that risen Christ to "easter in us, be a dayspring to the dimness of us, be a crimson-cresseted east."[51] That is above all why we celebrate Christian liturgy.

Notes

[1] San Francisco: Harper and Row, Publishers, 1979.

[2] For a Trinitarian intepretation of the liturgy, see Edward J. Kilmartin, *Christian Liturgy: Theology and Practice* (Kansas City: Sheed and Ward, 1988) 100-198; Jean Corbon, *The Wellspring of Worship*, trans. Matthew J. O'Connell (New York: Paulist, 1988).

[3] Enda McDonagh, *Invitation and Response: Essays in Christian Moral Theology* (Kansas City: Sheed and Ward, 1972) 96-97. The author addresses the relationship between liturgy and moral theology in several other works: *Doing the Truth: The Quest for Moral Theology* (Notre Dame: University of Notre Dame, 1979) 40-57, 58-75; *The Making of Disciples: Tasks of Moral Theology* (Wilmington: Glazier, 1982) 38-59, 99-111; *Between Chaos and New Creation: Doing Theology at the Fringe* (Wilmington: Glazier, 1986) 76-88.

[4] For a contemporary theology of the Trinity see Anthony Kelly, *The Trinity of Love: A Theology of the Christian God* (Wilmington: Glazier, 1989); William J. Hill, *The Three-Personed God: The Trinity as a Mystery of Salvation* (Washington: The Catholic University of America, 1982); Walter Kasper, *The God of Jesus Christ* (New York: Crossroad, 1984); John J. O'Donnell, *The Mystery of the Triune God* (London: Sheed and Ward, 1988); Leonardo Boff, *Trinity and Society* (Maryknoll, NY: Orbis, 1988); Catherine Mowry La Cugna, "The Trinitarian Mystery of God," *Systematic Theology: Roman Catholic Perspectives*,

ed. Elizabeth Schüssler Fiorenza and John P. Galvin (Minneapolis: Fortress, 1991) 1:151-92.

[5]For a contemporary treatment of Christology see Walter Kasper, *Jesus the Christ* (New York: Paulist, 1976); Dermot Lane, *The Reality of Jesus* (New York: Paulist, 1975); idem, *Christ at the Centre: Selected Issues in Christology* (New York: Paulist, 1991); John Macquarrie, *Jesus Christ in Modern Thought* (London: SCM, 1990); Wolfhart Pannenberg, *Jesus—God and Man* (Philadelphia: Westminster, 1968); Karl Rahner, *Foundations of Christian Faith* (New York: Seabury, 1978); Edward Schillebeeckx, *Jesus: An Experiment in Christology* (New York: Seabury, 1979); idem, *Christ: The Experience of Jesus as Lord* (New York: Seabury, 1980).

[6]Cf. Acts 10:40; 13:30-33; Rom 6:3-11; 10:8-10.

[7]Peter Drilling, *Trinity and Ministry* (Minneapolis: Fortress, 1991) esp. 23-53.

[8]McDonagh, *Invitation and Response*, 97-98.

[9]See Brevard S. Childs, *Memory and Tradition in Israel* (London: SCM, 1962).

[10]See Carmine Di Sante, *Jewish Prayer: The Origins of Christian Liturgy* (New York: Paulist, 1991).

[11]Kilmartin, 141-43.

[12]Di Sante, 159-69.

[13]McDonagh, *Invitation and Response*, 98-101.

[14]Demetrius Dumm, *Flowers In the Desert: A Spirituality of the Bible* (New York: Paulist, 1987) 35-53.

[15]An account of the transformative power of suffering can be found in many contemporary autobiographies; especially moving are those by Mary Craig, *Blessing* (London: Hodder and Stoughton, 1979); Michael Mayme, *A Year Lost and Found* (London: Darton, Longman and Todd, 1987); Margaret Spufford, *Celebration* (London: Fount Paperbacks/Collins, 1989); Christopher de Vinck, *The Power of the Powerless* (London: Hodder and Stoughton, 1988).

[16]Quoted by Craig, 134.

[17]Craig, 135.

[18]Regis Duffy, *On Becoming Catholic: The Challenge of Christian Initiation* (San Francisco: Harper and Row, 1984); Aidan Kavanagh, *The Shape of Baptism* (New York: Pueblo, 1978); Kennan Osborne, *The Christian Sacraments of Initiation* (New York: Paulist, 1987).

[19]For a study of Spencer's work see Duncan Robinson, *Stanley Spencer: Visions from a Berkshire Village* (Oxford: Phaidon, 1979); Louise Collis, *A Private View of Stanley Spencer* (London: Heinemann, 1972).

[20]The pilgrimage into the life of Christ is set out in a helpful way by Alan W. Jones in his books *Journey into Christ* (New York: Seabury, 1977); *Soul Making: The Desert Way of Spirituality* (San Francisco: Harper and Row, 1985); *Passion for Pilgrimage: Notes for the Journey Home* (San Francisco: Harper and Row, 1989).

[21] Cited by Jones, *Journey into Christ*, 54. See *The World of Charles Addams*, with intro. by Wilfred Sheed (New York: Knopf, 1991).

[22] Isa 55:1.

[23] See Louis Dupré, *Transcendent Selfhood: The Rediscovery of the Inner Life* (New York: Seabury, 1976) 42–46.

[24] "Conversation at Tea, 7," *The Avenue Bearing the Initial of Christ into the New World* (Boston: Houghton Mifflin, 1974) 33.

[25] Dianne Bergant, "Liturgy and Scripture: Creating a New World," *Liturgy and Social Justice*, ed. Edward M. Grosz (Collegeville: The Liturgical Press, 1988) 17–25.

[26] See Peter L. Berger, *The Social Reality of Religion* (London: Penguin, 1973); Mary Douglas and Steven Tipton, eds., *Religion and America: Spiritual Life in a Secular Age* (Boston: Beacon, 1983); David Martin, *A General Theory of Secularisation* (Oxford: Basil Blackwell, 1978).

[27] R. H. Blyth, *Haiku* (Tokyo: Hokuseido, 1952) 219.

[28] McDonagh, *Invitation and Response*, 101–03.

[29] Kieran Flanagan, *Sociology and Liturgy: Re-presentations of the Holy* (London: Macmillan, 1991); Andrew Greeley, *Unsecular Man: The Persistence of Religion* (New York: Dell, 1982); idem, *Religion: A Secular Theory* (New York: Free Press, 1982); Peter Williams, *Popular Religion: Symbolic Change and the Modernization Process in Historical Perspective* (Englewood Cliffs: Prentice-Hall, 1980).

[30] Aidan Kavanagh, *On Liturgical Theology* (New York: Pueblo Books, 1984); Tom O. Driver, *The Magic of Ritual* (San Francisco: Harper and Row, 1991).

[31] "Renewal: Ever Ancient, Ever New," *The Changing Face of Jewish and Christian Worship in North America*, ed. Paul F. Bradshaw and Lawrence A. Hoffman (Notre Dame: Univeristy of Notre Dame, 1991) 163.

[32] Ibid., 166.

[33] (New York: Pantheon Books, 1958) 175.

[34] See Gerhard Lohfink, *The Word of God Goes On* (Philadelphia: Fortress, 1987); Walter Brueggemann, Sharon Parks, and Thomas H. Groome, *To Act Justly, Love Tenderly, Walk Humbly: An Agenda for Ministers* (New York: Paulist, 1986); James Empereur and Christopher Kiesling, *The Liturgy That Does Justice: A New Approach to Liturgical Praxis* (Collegeville: The Liturgical Press/Michael Glazier Books, 1991); Kathleen Hughes and Mark R. Francis, eds., *Living No Longer for Ourselves: Liturgy and Justice in the Nineties* (Collegeville: The Liturgical Press, 1991); McDonagh, *The Making of Disciples*, 99–111.

[35] See Raymond E. Brown, *The Gospel According to John* (Garden City: Doubleday, 1970) 558; Oscar Cullmann, *Early Christian Worship* (London: SCM, 1953) 46–55, 105–10; Sandra M. Schneiders, "The Foot Washing (John 13:1-20): An Experiment in Hermeneutics," *The Catholic Biblical Quarterly* 43 (January 1981) 76–92.

[36] Mark Searle, "On Gestures," *Liturgy* 7 (December 1982–January 1983) 49–59.

[37] "On Ritual Knowledge," *Journal of Religion* 62 (1982) 111–27.
[38] Ibid., 115.
[39] Ibid., 116.
[40] See the articles in *Living No Longer for Ourselves: Liturgy and Justice in the Nineties,* eds. Kathleen Hughes and Mark R. Francis (Collegeville: The Liturgical Press, 1991); also William H. Willimon, *The Service of God: How Worship and Ethics are Related* (Nashville: Abingdon, 1983); Timothy F. Sedgwick, *Sacramental Ethics: Paschal Identity and the Christian Life* (Philadelphia: Fortress, 1987).
[41] Thomas F. O'Meara, *Fundamentalism: A Catholic Perspective* (New York: Paulist, 1990) 5–20.
[42] Peter Fink, *Worship: Praying the Sacraments* (Washington: Pastoral Press, 1991) 137–63.
[43] Ibid., 152. See also Theresa Koernke, "Towards an Ethic of Liturgical Behavior," *Worship* 66 (January 1992) 25–38.
[44] Jennings, 118–19.
[45] This was a point made by Cyprian in the third century: *On the Lord's Prayer,* no. 11, in *St Cyprian on the Lord's Prayer,* trans. J. Herbert Bindley (London: SPCK, 1914) 5:450.
[46] Jennings, 118.
[47] See for example Kenneth Untener, "Forum: The Ordination of Women: Can the Horizons Widen?" *Worship* 65 (1991) 50–59; Charles R. Meyer and Sara Butler, "Forum: The Ordination of Women: Responses to Bishop Kenneth Untener," *Worship* 65 (1991) 256–68; John R. Sheets, "Forum: The Ordination of Women," *Worship* 65 (1991) 451–61; Hervé Legrand, *"Traditio perpetuo servata?* The Non-ordination of Women: Tradition or Simply an Historical Fact?" *Worship* 65 (1991) 482–508.
[48] John 13:34-35.
[49] Isa 49-55; 66:10-14.
[50] (June 1987) 15–19.
[51] "The Wreck of the Deutschland," *The Norton Anthology of Modern Poetry,* ed. Richard Ellmann and Robert O'Clair (New York: W. W. Norton, 1973) 80.

5

In Praise of *Centesimus Annus*

Stanley M. Hauerwas

On Not Burying the Encyclical Tradition

I wrote an essay in response to John Paul II's *Laborem exercens* called, "Work as Co-Creation: A Critique of a Remarkably Bad Idea." In the first paragraph I said:

> A great chorus of praise has greeted Pope John Paul's encyclical, *Laborem exercens,* but I cannot join it. *Laborem exercens* is a disaster both in the general perspective it takes toward work as well as its specific arguments. I wish I could find a way to interpret the encyclical in a positive manner, but I find I cannot. My disease with this encyclical goes deeper, however, since the problem with *Laborem exercens* may well signal the end of the social encyclical tradition that began with Leo III's *Rerum novarum*. For it glaringly reveals the methodological shortcomings inherent in the encyclicals from their beginning.[1]

By "methodological shortcomings" I meant the abstract nature of encyclical pronouncements. The encyclical by necessity must be written at such a generalized level that their pronouncements seem platitudinous and irrelevant for policy decision. Moreover, the encyclicals of the past have often been based on "natural law" presuppositions that underwrite the abstract character of their discourse. As a result, I contended, the encyclicals were giving the impression that the Church, at least through the magisterial office, could speak in an a-historical fashion for all times and places.

I write as one who has to eat his words. For even though I do not think I was wrong about *Laborem exercens* (though I might have interpreted it in a more charitable light), I have to say that I think *Centesimus annus* is a worthy successor to *Rerum novarum*. Coming from me this is high praise in that I believe that *Rerum novarum* marks the high point of the social encyclical tradition; for *Rerum novarum* was written before Catholics, and in particular the popes, felt obliged to make their peace with modernity and in particular with liberalism.

What I like about *Rerum novarum*, in other words, is its anachronistic character. Leo XIII still pictured himself as a priest of a large parish, called "Christendom." He unapologetically set about showing where things had gone wrong by appealing to principles such as the just wage in a way that was remarkably premodern, as if Europe needed and wanted, and would readily receive, the pastoral care of the Church. Many years ago in a response to a paper by Charles Curran which praised the later encyclicals in opposition to *Rerum novarum*, I pointed out that Leo XIII and Karl Marx were friends.[2] Both were fundamentally conservative radicals challenging the kind of society being produced by the development of industrial capitalism. They rightly saw such developments as destroying any form of community that can sustain a sense of human solidarity. In Leo's case, of course, any account of human solidarity depended on the acknowledgement that what we share in common is our worship of God. Thus, in *Rerum novarum* Leo reminds state authorities and owners of their duty to provide for Sabbath observance as well as feast days so workers can go to Mass. He writes as a concerned pastor.

What I like about *Centesimus* is that it assumes a similar posture. I cannot deny that *Centesimus* accepts more from the later encyclicals than I would like, but in many ways I think it could signal a return to the radical ecclesial vision of *Rerum novarum*. Therefore, I will focus my remarks on this new encyclical with some reference to *Rerum novarum*. I had originally intended to concentrate on *Rerum novarum*, but this new encyclical is so interesting that by concentrating on it we may be able to grasp once again Leo XIII's insistence that the foremost social witness of the Church for the world is our worship of God. The assumption at work here is unmistakable and profound: it is the Church, and the Church alone, which provides the world with the means to know the substance of the good society.[3]

On Historical Modesty and Ethical Judgment

One of the attractive features of *Centesimus* is the modesty of its claims. Much has been made of John Paul II's praise of market economies, but more important, I think, is his statement in *Centesimus* that

> The church has no models to present; models that are real and truly effective can only arise within the framework of different historical situations through the efforts of all those who responsibly confront concrete problems in all their social, economic, political and cultural aspects as these interact with one another. For such a task the church offers her social teaching as an indispensable and ideal orientation, a teaching which, as already mentioned, recognizes the positive value of the market and of enterprise, but which at the same time points out that these need to be oriented toward the common good (43).[4]

The Pope does not invite us to speculate about a "third way" between capitalism and socialism. The issues before us are far more important than that choice suggested since what is at stake is not an alternative "model" of economics the Church can put forward, but rather how the Church stands as an alternative to all such models. In effect, the Pope's modesty about economics is based on his rightful immodesty about the significance of the Church.

It is exactly this "immodesty" in *Centesimus*, in contrast to more recent encyclicals, that seems to free John Paul II to argue in an historical and concrete manner. Not only do we get a remarkably specific account of the 1989 revolution, but the encyclical explicitly acknowledges the more general point that history and truth are not incompatible categories. Thus, the Pope contends that the Church does not close

> her eyes to danger of fanaticism or fundamentalism among those who, in the name of an ideology which purports to be scientific or religious, claim the right to impose on others their own concept of what is true and good. Christian truth is not of this kind. Since it is not an ideology, the Christian faith does not presume to imprison changing sociopolitical realities in a rigid schema, and it recognizes that human life is realized in history in conditions that are diverse and imperfect.

The crucial thing to note here is that these reflections are the product of a Church that is confronting the contingencies of history.

Of course the trick is to work in a historicist perspective without translating "what is" into "what ought to be," without, in other words, underwriting the prevailing economic order by declaring its particular patterns of production and consumption as normative, something that both Leo XIII and John Paul II went to great lengths to avoid.

On this score, there is some slippage in the encyclical. It is one thing to say the Church has no economic theory, but the very way the Pope describes current economic options may betray such a theory. For example, in the context of developing a quite powerful critique of how modern economic developments destroy our ability to welcome children into our midst, we are told that these criticisms are directed not so much against an economic system as against an ethical and cultural system:

> The economy in fact is only one aspect and one dimension of the whole of human activity. If economic life is absolutized, if the production and consumption of goods become the center of social life and society's only value, not subject to any other value, the reason is to be found not so much in the economic system itself as in the fact that the entire sociocultural system, by ignoring the ethical and religious dimension, has been weakened and ends by limiting itself to the production of goods and services alone (39).

The problem here is that the Pope's attempt to distinguish the economic from the political and cultural system may reflect the very liberal ideology that in other contexts the encyclical means to challenge. For it is liberalism that tries to make the economic realm an independent realm determined by its own laws and processes. Indeed, such a presumption is the basis for the idea that economics is a science that is separable from politics and ethics. This presumption, it seems to me, is exactly what *Rerum novarum* rightly challenged by making central just wage as the criteria for good economic relations. For the "just wage" is determined by calculating what is required for the sustaining of families and children, not by the exigencies of the autonomous market.

Of course, the case can be made that the distinction between "the economic" and "the cultural" may simply be a way for the Pope to remind us that those activities we name as economic are in service to move determinative goods. But by so humbling the "economic," it is important that such humility does not become an idealogy for capitalism. For example, if economics are to be judged by the service they provide for the flowering of the family then it might well mean that we must challenge the tendency of the modern corporation to make efficiency the criteria of good business.

One of the ways that John Paul II avoids abstractions such as capitalism and socialism is by focusing on the nature of work. Work becomes the hermeneutical key to reveal the character of any regime. In other words, John Paul II rightly sees that the way to avoid overly formal and ultimately false alternatives is by forcing us to look concretely at what is actually happening to people. In this respect the encyclical stands in the tradition of *Rerum novarum* and *Laborem exercens*. Here, however, John Paul II gives an account of the communal dimension of work that puts the emphasis on the "creative" aspect of work in *Laborem exercens* in a new perspective; thus he notes, "It is becoming clearer how a person's work is naturally interrelated with the work of others. More than ever, work is work with others and work for others: It is a matter of doing something for someone else" (31). Later we are reminded that "by means of his work man commits himself not only for his own sake, but also for others and with others. Each person collaborates in the work of others and for their good" (43). Thus John Paul II reminds us that what is crucial is not that our work in and of itself is "creative," but rather that it is of service to others—i.e., let us praise those who pick up our trash and clean our offices.

The power of this perspective is illustrated by another East European leader who also compels us to look at labor not in the abstract but in the concrete, Vaclav Havel. In an essay on *Living in Truth* entitled "The Power of the Powerless," Havel tells the following story:

> In 1974, when I was employed in a brewery, my immediate superior was a certain *s*, a person well versed in the art of making beer. He was proud of his profession and he wanted our brew-

ery to brew good beer. He spent almost all his time at work, continually thinking up improvements and he frequently made the rest of us feel uncomfortable because he assumed that we loved brewing as much as he did. In the midst of the slovenly indifference to work that socialism encourages, a more constructive worker would be difficult to imagine.

The brewery itself was managed by people who understood their work less and were less fond of it, but who were politically more influential. They were bringing the brewery to ruin and not only did they fail to react to any of *s*'s suggestions, but they actually became increasingly hostile towards him and tried in every way to thwart his efforts to do a good job. Eventually the situation became so bad that *s* felt compelled to write a lengthy letter to the manager's superior, in which he attempted to analyze the brewery's difficulties. He explained why it was the worst in the district and pointed to those responsible.

His voice might have been heard. The manager, who was politically powerful but otherwise ignorant of beer, a man who loathed workers and was given to intrigue, might have been replaced and conditions in the brewery might have been improved on the basis of *s*'s suggestions. Had this happened, it would have been a perfect example of small-scale work in action. Unfortunately the precise opposite occurred: the manager of the brewery, who was a member of the Communist Party's district committee, had friends in higher places and he saw to it that the situation was resolved in his favour. *S*'s analysis was a "defamatory document" and *s* himself was "political saboteur." He was thrown out of the brewery and shifted to another one where he was given a job requiring no skill. Here the notion of small-scale work had come up against the wall of the post-totalitarian system. By speaking the truth, *s* had stepped out of line, broken the rules, cast himself out, and he ended up as a sub-citizen, stigmatized as an enemy. He could now say anything he wanted, but he could never, as a matter of principle, expect to be heard. He had become the "dissident" of the Eastern Bohemian Brewery.[5]

John Paul II and Havel are reminding us that good societies are ones that encourage good brewers to brew good beer. Before neo-conservatives rejoice in the Popes acceptance of market economies, I think they might well ask whether in fact most capitalist societies are able to meet *Centesimus'* understanding of the moral character of work. For economic transactions cannot be "spiritually empty" if we are to serve one another and the goods thereby embodied.[6]

The fact that work has a moral purpose is something that "liberals" and "conservatives" forget. They become too enamored with issues of distribution. This is why John Paul II reminds us that "economics" is not just a matter of which economic systems can produce the most units to be more widely distributed, but what kind of people we become through those economic systems. How our work engenders trust in ourselves and others is surely more important than the assumption that good economics are those subject to constant growth.

Why Truth and Love Are More Important Than "Rights"

The great strength of this encyclical is that it directs us to the question, "what kind of moral habits and institutions are necessary to encourage good brewers to brew good beer?" It is on this score that *Centesimus* stands in such prominent continuity with *Rerum novarum* and its critique of liberalism. Specifically, in contrast to more recent encyclicals the liberal language of "rights" in *Centesimus* is distinctly muted. Certainly "rights" are still used to mark important goods, but the notion that rights are primarily moral notions is clearly rejected.

Rights are subordinate to prior obligation.[7] But the specification of such obligation requires an understanding of goods that are more than simply an appeal to the right of the individual to make up his or her own mind.[8] Put in terms of *Rerum novarum,* this encyclical assumes that truth is prior to any account of rights. As John Paul II says:

> Finally, development must not be understood solely in economic terms, but in a way that is fully human. It is not only a question of raising all peoples to the level currently enjoyed by the richest countries, but rather of building up a more decent life through united labor, of concretely enhancing every individual's dignity and creativity as well as his capacity to respond to his personal vocation and thus to God's call. The apex of development is the exercise of the right and duty to seek God, to know him and to live in accordance with that knowledge. In the totalitarian and

authoritarian regimes, the principle that force predominates over reason was carried to the extreme. Man was compelled to submit to a conception of reality imposed on him by coercion and not reached by virtue of his own reason and the exercise of his own freedom. This principle must be overturned and total recognition must be given to the rights of the human conscience, which is bound only to the truth, both natural and revealed. The recognition of these rights represents the primary foundation of every authentically free political order (29).

Here we see the traditional claim that freedom is not and cannot be an end in itself. Rather, freedom is subordinate to the discernment and articulation of truth. Thus, the Pope assumes that so called "free speech" is "free" only insofar as it is in service to a more profound good. Christians are not about the creation of "free" societies, but rather of societies in which people can worship the true God truthfully. All that we do depends on our wills being rightly directed to the One who alone is worthy of worship.

Of course, this creates a problem about the status of the Church in liberal societies, but it is far better to recognize this as a continuing problem than to assume that it can easily be solved by some false notion such as "freedom of religion." The Pope rightly knows that Roman Catholicism is not "a religion" in an abstract sense, but rather a people committed to the evangelization of the social orders in which it finds itself. There is no question, therefore, of the Church being pushed aside into a private personal realm in the name of "freedom of conscience." The Church cannot, in the name of becoming "free," underwrite a social policy that makes it a matter of indifference whether one worships or does not worship God.

By emphasizing the organic relationship between the Church and society, John Paul II stands in deep continuity with Leo XIII. In this regard one of my favorite passages in *Rerum novarum* (22) is:

> Of these things there cannot be the shadow of doubt; for instance, that civil society was renovated in every part by the teachings of Christianity; that in the strength of that renewal the human race was lifted up to better things—nay, that it was brought back from death to life, and to so excellent a life that nothing more perfect had been known before or will come to pass in the ages that are yet to be. Of this beneficent transformation, Jesus Christ was at once the first cause and the final pur-

pose; as from Him all came, so to Him all was to be referred. For when, by the light of the Gospel message, the human race came to know the grand mystery of the Incarnation of the Word and the redemption of man, the life of Jesus Christ, God and Man, penetrated every race and nation, and impregnated them with His faith, His precepts, and His laws. And, if Society is to be cured now, in no other way can it be cured but by a return to the Christian life and Christian institutions. When a Society is perishing, the true advice to give to those who would restore it is, to recall it to the principles from which it sprung; for the purpose and perfection of an association is to aim at and to attain that for which it was formed; and its operation should be put in motion and inspired by the end and object which originally gave it its being. So that to fall away from its primal constitution is disease; to go back to it is recovery. And this may be asserted with the utmost truth both of the State in general and of that body of its citizens—by far the greatest number—who sustain life by labor.

Thus, in response to the ills of modern industrial society, Leo XIII prescribed the only true cure, "a return to Christian life and Christian institutions." I am aware such claims tend to make Catholics in America squeamish, but there is no way around them if we are to honestly hold, with Leo XIII, that truth derives from truthful worship.[9]

Think, for example, of what this means for how Christians might conceive of social policies concerning divorce. In *Costi connubii* Pius XI maintained that "it is clear that marriage even in the state of nature, and certainly long before it was raised to the dignity of a sacrament, was divinely instituted in such a way that it should carry with it a perpetual and indissoluble bond which cannot therefore be dissolved by any civil law."[10] I am not suggesting that such a position would necessarily commit the Church to one social policy concerning basic issues like marriage and divorce, but at the very least it means that any policy must be based on more than what is socially expedient or "good" for individuals.

It is in regard to such concrete matters as these that the encyclical tradition stands in continuing tension with the presuppositions of liberal democracy. Liberal democracies are both justified and formed on the presumption that no one knows the truth or, to put it perhaps more charitably, that whatever we mean by "truth" can only be discovered through the "marketplace of ideas." Yet neither Leo XIII nor John Paul II can make their peace with any such presumptions nor with any societies so constituted. Indeed, John Paul II reminds us that at the heart of the Church's vision of the social good is the principle of solidarity. "This principle is frequently stated by Pope Leo XIII, who uses the term *friendship*, a concept already found in Greek philosophy. Pope Pius XI refers to it with the equally meaningful term *social charity*. Pope Paul VI, expanding the concept to cover the many modern aspects of the social question speaks of a civilization of love" (10).

Such language may appear foolish or naive in the face of our so called political realities, but I think there can be no greater realism. For example, the analysis of Havel is not dissimilar. He notes the crisis facing the societies of the west in that our technologies are out of control. Hoping to use technique as a substitute for genuine community, the "freedom" acquired through technique has enslaved us and compelled us to participate in the preparation of our own destruction. Moreover, there is, according to Havel, no evidence that democracies of the West (of traditional parliamentary type) offer any solution. Indeed, Havel suggests

> that the more room there is in the Western democracies (compared to our world) for the genuine aims of life, the better the crisis is hidden from people and the more deeply do they become immersed in it.
>
> It would appear that the traditional parliamentary democracies can offer no fundamental opposition to the automatism of technological civilization and the industrial-consumer society, for they, too, are being dragged helplessly along by it. People are manipulated in ways that are infinitely more subtle and refined than the brutal methods used in the post-totalitarian societies. But this static complex of rigid, conceptually sloppy and politically pragmatic mass political parties run by professional apparatuses and releasing the citizen from all forms of concrete and personal responsibility; and those complex focuses of capital accumulation engaged in secret manipulations and expansion; the omnipresent dictatorship of consumption, production, advertising, commerce, consumer culture, and all that flood of information: all of it, so often analyzed and described, can only with great difficulty be imagined as the source of humanity's rediscovery of itself. In his June 1978 Harvard lecture, Solzhenitsyn

describes the illusory nature of freedoms not based on personal responsibility and the chronic inability of the traditional democracies, as a result, to oppose violence and totalitarianism. In a democracy, human beings may enjoy many personal freedoms and securities that are unknown to us, but in the end they do them no good, for they too are ultimately victims of the same automatism, and are incapable of defending their concerns about their own identity or preventing their superficialization or transcending concerns about their own personal survival to become proud and responsible members of the polis, making a genuine contribution to the creation of its destiny.[11]

Thus Havel asks the question, What then are we to do? And in a language not far from John Paul II, he answers by suggesting that all of us, East and West, have one fundamental task from which all else follows:

That task is one of resisting vigilantly, thoughtfully and attentively, but at the same time with total dedication, at every step and everywhere, the irrational momentum of anonymous, impersonal and inhuman power—the power of ideologies, systems, *apparat,* bureaucracy, artificial languages and political slogans. We must resist their complex and wholly alienating pressure, whether it takes the form of consumption, advertising, repression, technology, or cliché—all of which are the blood brothers of fanaticism and the wellspring of totalitarian thought. We must draw our standards from our natural world, heedless of ridicule, and reaffirm its denied validity. We must honour with the humility of the wise the bounds of that natural world and the mystery which lies beyond them, admitting that there is something in the order of being which evidently exceeds all our competence; relating ever again to the absolute horizon of our existence which, if we but will, we shall constantly rediscover and experience; making values and imperatives into the starting point of all our acts, of all our personally attested, openly contemplated and ideologically uncensored lived experience. We must trust the voice of our conscience more than that of all abstract speculations and not invent other responsibilities than the one to which the voice calls us. We must not be ashamed that we are capable of love, friendship, solidarity, sympathy and tolerance, but just the opposite: we must set these fundamental dimensions of our humanity free from their "private" exile and accept them as the only genuine starting point of meaningful human community.

We must be guided by our own reason and serve the truth under all circumstances as our own essential experience.[12]

Because John Paul II and Havel share the presumption that good societies are finally about truth, they refuse to accept liberal nostrums for social problems.

For example, John Paul II rightly resists formalistic appeals to economic justice as a solution to poverty (57). The poor will not be served by empowering them to become consumers. Indeed, the Pope insightfully suggests that liberalism is an attempt to defeat Marxism by its own form of materialism, that is, through the creation of needs without any concept of our true good:

> A given culture reveals its overall understanding of life through the choices it makes in production and consumption. It is here that the phenomenon of consumerism arises. In singling out new needs and new means to meet them, one must be guided by a comprehensive picture of man which respects all the dimensions of his being and which subordinates his material and instinctive dimensions to his interior and spiritual ones. If, on the contrary, a direct appeal is made to his instincts—while ignoring in various ways the reality of the person as intelligent and free—then consumer attitudes and lifestyles can be created which are objectively improper and often damaging to his physical and spiritual health. Of itself, an economic system does not possess criteria for correctly distinguishing new and higher forms of satisfying human needs from artificial new needs which hinder the formation of a mature personality. Thus a great deal of education and cultural work is urgently needed, including the education of consumers in the responsible use of their power of choice, the formation of a strong sense of responsibility among producers and among people in the mass media in particular as well as the necessary intervention by public authorities (36).

The question, of course, is how we can be so educated in the midst of market economies since they generate exactly the kind of consumer demand that he sees is at the heart of the problem. Thus, John Paul II reminds us that the economy cannot do this alone but depends on educational and cultural forces. Yet such strategies seem undermined by the capacity of market economics to subordinate everything to issues of economic rationality. So we need to know more about what should be left outside market forces.

For example, should we allow blood to be bought and sold?[13] Or to put it in the most offensive possible way, there is no question that the *Centesimus* like *Rerum novarum* is about the subordination of the economic and political orders to love.

The question, particularly in liberal societies, is how that is to be done. Liberal societies train us to believe that our own self-interest is legitimate, that our greed through market mechanism serves the common good. But that "good" turns out to be little more than an aggregate of our self-interests. For those of us produced by such societies to speak about love and economics surely sounds like madness. Yet John Paul II has profoundly challenged such societies. And for that we are in his debt. The question remains, however, what alternative do we have?

The Violence of Economics

It is exactly in relation to this kind of question that the history of the revolution of 1989 provided in chapter III of the encyclical is so important. This is a new development in the encyclical tradition that bodes well for the future. For it is nothing less than a theological commentary on the developments in Eastern Europe from World War II to the present. It is at once the source that shapes the moral vision of the encyclical and the central example that gives power to that vision. Through that history John Paul II criticizes socialism for its assumption that the individual person is simply "an element, a molecule within the social organism so that the good of the individual is completely subordinated to the functioning of the socioeconomic mechanism" (13). This is a old and rather tired argument. But the Pope deepens the point by arguing that lurking behind this reduction of the human person is, quite bluntly, atheism. Moreover, it is not just any atheism, but the atheism born of the rationalism of the Enlightenment "which views human and social reality in a mechanistic way" (13).

Such atheism, according to John Paul II, is the source of the socialist presumption that societies are caught in unavoidable class conflicts. Moreover, such a presumption is also the source of the militarism of modern societies:

> In a word, it is a question of transferring to the sphere of internal conflict between social groups the doctrine of "total war,"

which the militarism and imperialism of that time brought to bear on international relations. As a result of this doctrine, the search for a proper balance between the interests of the various nations was replaced by attempts to impose the absolute domination of one's own side through the destruction of the other side's capacity to resist, using every possible means, not excluding the use of lies, terror tactics against citizens and weapons of utter destruction (which precisely in those years were beginning to be designed). Therefore class struggle in the Marxist sense and militarism have the same root, namely, atheism and contempt for the human person, which place the principle of force above that of reason and law (14).

Given the Pope's own experience of Poland, it is not surprising that his analysis in this regard is primarily directed at socialism. Yet capitalism is based on the same atheistic presupposition he finds in socialism. Moreover, capitalist societies have been at least as militaristic as socialist societies, if not more. Both capitalist and socialist societies are predicated in violence. And both are legitimated by modernist social theories which, as John Milbank has argued in his stunning *Theology and Social Theory,* are grounded in the assumption that violence and not peace (which the Pope calls "love") is the basic characteristic of the human condition.[14] Milbank argues, I think rightly, that the social world that secular economics and sociology "describes" and thereby makes appear inevitable, is the very condition that produced the social sciences as legitimating forms of thought for the liberal project. Thus, social sciences can pretend to possess predictive power exactly because they train us to act as individuals in competition with other individuals for survival.

In this respect we might have wished that the Pope would have been more critical of the so-called free or market societies. As Herbert McCabe, O.P., has pointed out to me, the Pope goes to great lengths to suggest that there are many different kinds of market societies, e.g., distinguishing between market and capitalist societies, but he does not in similar fashion make it clear that socialism is equally diverse. It would have been even more helpful if the Pope had developed his criticism of the rationalism of the Enlightenment to suggest how we are all now caught in alternatives that presume the necessity of violence.

That is why I think the Pope's account of the history of Eastern Europe so important. For he tells that story as the story of the triumph of truth and love over violence. "It seemed," the Pope writes

> that the European order resulting from World War II and sanctioned by the Yalta agreements could only be overturned by another war. Instead, it has been overcome by the non-violent commitment of people who, while always refusing to yield to the force of power, succeeded time after time in finding effective ways of bearing witness to the truth. This disarmed the adversary, since violence always needs to justify itself through deceit and to appear, however falsely, to be defending a right or responding to a threat posed by others. Once again I thank God for having sustained people's hearts amid difficult trials, and I pray that this example will prevail in other places and other circumstances. May people learn to fight for justice without violence, renouncing class struggle in their internal disputes and war in international ones (23).

By no means has the Pope become a pacifist, but this testimony is unmistakable in its significance. For the Pope is suggesting that Christians best serve the societies in which we find ourselves by developing habits of truth and non-violence.

For Havel, too, truth and non-violence are the power of the powerless, for only through truth can we resist the lies that are the source of violence. Such truth may be as simple as a green grocer in a socialist society refusal to display in his or her shop window the sign "Workers of the world unite." As Havel points out, to display such a sign seems harmless in and of itself, but the green grocer knows it to be a lie that confirms the surrounding presumption that socialism is a workers paradise. Exactly because so little seems to be at stake in such a display, those who put the sign in their window lose their hold on the truth and submit to the order of violence.[15] Similarly, John Paul II, through his narrative of Eastern Europe, invites us to become part of God's people by refusing to submit to violent narratives that capture our souls by asking us to submit to false economic and political orders through seemingly meaningless and insignificant acts—acts like putting yellow ribbons on church doors.

On Theological History

The striking account of the revolution in Eastern Europe of 1989 reflects the theological method employed in the encyclical. I have said little about these matters to this point because I think *Centesimus* is distinguished exactly in that it does not concentrate on "method." There are simply no extended discussions of natural law. Instead, the Pope unapologetically works with explicit theological categories.

Thus, the Pope makes clear, in contra-distinction to liberal Christian theologians such as Reinhold Niebuhr, that sin is first and foremost a theological claim. We only know we are sinners because we have been revealed so by Christ. The Pope writes that

> man, who was created for freedom, bears within himself the wound of original sin, which constantly draws him toward evil and puts him in need of redemption. Not only is this doctrine an integral part of Christian revelation, it also has great hermeneutical value insofar as it helps one to understand human reality. Man tends toward good, but he is also capable of evil. He can transcend his immediate interest and still remain bound to it. The social order will be all the more stable, the more it takes this fact into account and does not place in opposition personal interest and the interests of society as a whole, but rather seeks ways to bring them into fruitful harmony. In fact, where self-interest is violently suppressed, it is replaced by a burdensome system of bureaucratic control which dries up the wellsprings of initiative and creativity. When people think they possess the secret of a perfect social organization which makes evil impossible, they also think that they can use any means, including violence and deceit, in order to bring that organization into being. Politics then becomes a "secular religion" which operates under the illusion of creating paradise in this world (25).

That is why the Pope describes *Rerum novarum* as part of the Church's evangelizing mission (54). For what we have here is no independent anthropology that can be known by anyone apart from Christological claims. In the encyclicals the Church

> proclaims God and his mystery or salvation in Christ to every human being and for that very reason reveals man to himself. In this light, and only in this light, does it concern itself with

everything else: the human rights of the individual and in particular of the "working class," the family and education, the duties of the state, the ordering of national and international society, economic life, culture, war and peace and respect for life from the moment of conception until death (54).

There is no "natural law" minimalism in this encyclical. There is no false humility about the place of the Church in society or the correlative theological task. Rather, the Pope boldly and rightly calls our attention to those whose lives only make sense in light of the God who is disclosed in the life, death, and resurrection of Jesus of Nazareth. It is as the basis of that Christian witness that the Pope can write the history of 1989 as the triumph over violence of truth and love.

Of course, that triumph came only through the willingness of many to suffer. The Pope does not avoid the question of suffering. On the contrary, he writes that

> in following Christ demands to be communicated to other people in their concrete difficulties, struggles, problems and challenges, so that these can then be illuminated and made more human in the light of faith. Faith not only helps people to find solutions; it makes even situations of suffering humanly bearable, so that in these situations people will not become lost or forget their dignity and vocation (59).[16]

Yet finally, one might have hoped that the Pope would have developed this theme of suffering with the depth of Leo XIII in an encyclical promulgated one year after *Rerum novarum*. The encyclical was entitled *Rosary and Social Question*.[17] In it Leo XIII noted that one of the greatest evils gripping modern social order is a repugnance to any kind of suffering. He lamented that as a result most people

> are thus robbed of that peace and freedom of mind which remains the reward of those who do what is right, undismayed by the perils or troubles to be met with in doing so. Rather do they dream of a chimeric civilization in which all that is unpleasant shall be removed, and all that is pleasant shall be supplied. By this passionate and unbridled desire of living a life of pleasure, the minds of men are weakened, and if they do not entirely suc-

cumb, they become demoralized and miserably cower and sink under the hardships of the battle of life (4).

I know of no more prophetic words for our times, and no more effective analyses of the ills that afflict societies like the United States of America. As a remedy Leo XIII directed our attention to Christ:

> We see Him bound like a malefactor, subjected to the judgement of the unrighteous, laden with insults, covered with shame, assailed with false accusations, torn with scourges, crowned with thorns, nailed to the cross, accounted unworthy to live, and condemned by the voice of the multitude as deserving of death. Here, too, we contemplate the grief of the Most Holy Mother, whose soul was not only wounded but "pierced" (John 19:37) by the sword of sorrow, so that she might be named and become in truth "the Mother of Sorrows." Witnessing these examples of fortitude, not with sight but by faith, who is there who will not feel his heart grow warm with the desire of imitating them?
> Then, be it that the "earth is accursed" and brings forth "thistles and thorns" (Gen. 3:14), be it that the soul is saddened with grief and the body with sickness; even so, there will be no evil which the envy of man or the rage of the devils can invent, nor calamity which can fall upon the individual or the community, over which we shall not triumph by the patience of suffering. For this reason it has been truly said that "it belongs to the Christian to do and to endure great things," for he who deserves to be called a Christian must not shrink from following in the footsteps of Christ. But by this patience, We do not mean the empty stoicism in the enduring of pain which was the ideal of some of the philosophers of old, but rather do We mean that patience which is learned from the example of Him, who "having joy set before him, endured the cross, despising the shame" (Heb 12:2). It is the patience which is obtained by the help of His grace; which shirks not a trial because it is painful, but which accepts it and esteems it as a gain, however hard it may be to undergo. The Catholic Church has always had, and happily still has, multitudes of men and women, in every rank and condition of life, who are glorious disciples of this teaching, and who, following faithfully in the path of Christ, suffer injury and hardship for the cause of virtue and religion. They re-echo, not with their lips, but with their life, the words of St. Thomas: "Let us also go, that we may die with him" (John 11:16). May such types of admirable constancy be more and more splendidly multiplied in our midst to

the weal of society and to the glory and edification of the Church of God! (4)

No celebration of *Rerum novarum* is complete without these words of Leo XIII for they remind us that the virtue most necessary for the life of non-violence is that of patience, and that patience is formed by the life of prayer.[18]

Notes

[1] Stanley Hauerwas, "Work as Co-Creation: A Critique of a Remarkably Bad Idea," *Co-Creation and Capitalism: John Paul II's Laborem exercens,* John Houck and Oliver Williams, eds. (Washington: University Press of America, 1983) 42.

[2] "The Future of Christian Social Ethics," *That They May Live: Theological Reflection on the Quality of Life,* George Divine, ed. (Staten Island: Alba House, 1972) 123-131.

[3] John Colemann, S.J., drawing on the work of Michael Schuck, notes that it is a mistake to begin the history of modern Roman Catholic social pronouncements with *Rerum novarum*. Rather, one should begin with Gregory XVI's *Mirari vos* and Pius IX's *Quanta cura* and *The Syllabus of Errors*. In other words, the social encyclicals are really a response to the "French Revolution and the rise of the new bourgeois liberties with the doctrine of separation of church and state." According to Colemann, Schuck argues that there is a coherence to the social encyclical tradition from 1740 to the present that is constituted by the popes construal of the world as a medium of God's ubiquity. Whether pictured as a positive, a cosmos, or unmarked path, the world is imbued with God's presence. Monika Hellwig [Schuck notes] discusses this characteristically Roman Catholic perspective when she says: "There is no realms whatsoever outside the dimensions of that God." She continues, "Neither politics nor economics, neither national interests nor international affairs, neither technology nor commerce, neither aesthetics nor productivity, can ultimately be a law unto itself." As a result, the Popes uniformly criticize world views inspired by atheistic naturalism and dialectical materialism. (John Colemann, S.J. "A Tradition Celebrated, Reevaluated, and Applied," in *One Hundred Years of Catholic Social Thought,* John Colemann, ed. [Maryknoll: Orbis, 1991] 3-4.) The quote is from Schuck's dissertation, "The Context and Coherence of Roman Catholic Encyclical Social Teaching: 1740-1987," written at the Divinity School, University of Chicago, 1987.

I am sure that Schuck is right to contend that the tradition begins earlier than *Rerum novarum*. In effect, the social encyclicals are the product of the rise of papal supremacy that went hand in hand with the rise of the new nation state system. Those who criticize the development of "papal absolutism" often fail to appreciate that the increase of papal power, perhaps unconsciously, was necessary to counter the rise of nation-state absolutism. Schuck's important dissertation has recently been published as *That They Be One: The Social Teachings of the Papal Encyclicals 1740-1989* (Washington: Georgetown University Press, 1991).

[4] This translation of *Centesimus annus* is found in *Origins* 21 (May 16, 1991). All pagination of the paragraph numbers of the Encyclical will appear in the text.

[5] Vaclav Havel, *Living in Truth* (London: Faber, 1986) 82-83.

[6] Some neo-conservatives defend capitalism as entailing no moral implications by claiming that it is "spiritually empty."

[7] The obligation to earn one's bread by the sweat of one's brow also presumes the right to do so. A society in which this right is systematically denied, in which economic policies do not allow workers to reach satisfactory levels of employment, cannot be justified from an ethical point of view nor can that society attain social peace (43).

[8] It is certainly the case that John Paul II uses the language of "inalienable rights" (7), but such rights are always meant to suggest that "persons" have existence prior to the state. I am aware that such "rights" can lead to a form of liberal individualism, and there are certainly hints in this encyclical in that direction, but I think that God, not the person, stands more determinatively at the center of the Pope's vision.

[9] I love the fact that *Centesimus annus* has been published in Ireland and England by the *Catholic Truth Society*. I assume it is significant that this society rightly understands that truth is appropriately qualified by Catholic.

[10] Pius XI, *Costi connubii* in *Five Great Encyclicals* (New York: Paulist, 1939) par. 34.

[11] Havel, 115-116.

[12] Havel, 153-154.

[13] In several places in *Centesimus*, John Paul II makes clear that "there are collective and qualitative needs which cannot be satisfied by market mechanisms. There are important human needs which escape its logic. There are goods which by their very nature cannot and must not be bought or sold" (40). Yet the encyclical does not provide much help for discerning what should be excluded from the market.

[14] John Milbank, *Theology and Social Theory: Beyond Secular Reason* (Oxford: Basil Blackwell, 1990).

[15] Havel develops this example on pages 41-42 of *Living in Truth*.

[16] In commenting on the 1989 struggle, John Paul II notes "it was a struggle born of prayer, and it would have been unthinkable without immense trust in God, the Lord of history, who carries the human heart in his hands. It is by uniting his own sufferings for the sake of truth and freedom to the suffer-

ing of Christ on the cross than man is able to accomplish the miracle of peace and is in a position to discern the often narrow path between the cowardice which gives in to evil and the violence which under the illusion of fighting evil only makes it worse" (25).

[17] *The Rosary: A Social Remedy,* Thomas Schwertner, O.P., ed. (Milwaukee: Bruce, 1934) par. 4.

[18] I am indebted to Michael J. Baxter, C.S.C., for his critique and constructive suggestions for revising this paper. It is much better because of him.

6

The Ethical Imperative of the Eucharist: Responding in the Workplace

Regina Wentzel Wolfe

Understanding the Relation of Business and Morality

In the past twenty years we have witnessed an increasing awareness of and concern for questionable or unacceptable practices and activities in the workplace. Once infrequent, reports of misconduct on the part of corporations or their employees seem almost commonplace today. The insider trading scandals on Wall Street have made Ivan Boesky and Michael Milken household names. Three Mile Island and the Exxon Valdez tragedies highlight public concerns for the impact of big business on the environment. Acid rain, deforestation, and waste disposal methods are among a seemingly endless list of environmental concerns which confront business and industry. Questionable marketing techniques which led to the successful boycott of Nestlés S.A. still abound. Just ask the priests and ministers in New York, Chicago, and Los Angeles who whitewash billboards glamorizing cigarette and alcohol use in ads aimed at minority consumers and inner city youths. Health and safety issues underscore discussions on responsible operating procedures. Employment practices, wage policies, and employee rights and benefits are commonly included in discussions on corporate social responsibility.

Once the domain of academics and other specialists, the discussion of values and ethics in business has moved into the mainstream of American debate. Articles on corporate behavior and responsibility abound in both the popular press and specialized journals.

Members of the public are dissatisfied with how corporate America is managed. They seem to think that corporate managers have few, if any, ethical standards. There is certainly something odd about this conclusion. One of its implications is that the men and women who run our companies, if not immoral, are at best amoral. Most of us know people involved in business. Generally, however, we do not deem these friends and relatives to be bad people. In fact, we usually view them as good, honest, upstanding members of society who work hard and perform their jobs to the best of their ability. If this is the case, who are the unethical people in business? The answer can only be that it is the people we don't know who are the ruthless, uncaring, dishonest individuals responsible for the sorry state of business today. This does not seem to be a reasonable view, either.

Nevertheless, dissatisfaction with corporate America exists. This dissatisfaction is based on two widely held views. The first is that managers of large corporations are principally concerned with profits and a return on investment for stockholders. The second is that corporations and their managers only respond to the needs and concerns of others with a stake in the corporations when confronted with legislative constraints or when confronted with a potentially negative impact on corporate profitability.

This perception of business offers a bleak view of corporate America, its values, and the men and women who work there. I believe that it is a perception that is overly pessimistic and does not adequately acknowledge the complexities of the workplace and the generally honest and hardworking men and women found in it. It is important to note that there are two issues involved here. One concerns the personal ethics and values of individuals in the workplace. The other is more structural and deals with the manner in which corporations are managed and the ability of those who work in them to integrate ethical reflection into the decision making process. Thus, we must be concerned with a two-pronged approach when addressing ethical issues in business. We must be concerned with the individual person in the workplace as well as the structures with which he or she is confronted when attempting to find an answer for a particular ethical dilemma.

If we accept that most people in the business world are honest and act with moral integrity, what explanation is there for the negative perception of business and the resistance toward acknowledging that there is a place for ethics in the business world? Professor Richard De George, an expert in business ethics from the University of Kansas, suggests a reason for this resistance to acknowledging the relationship between business and ethics. There has existed in the United States what he calls the Myth of Amoral Business. According to this myth, those involved in business are amoral. They feel that moral considerations are inappropriate in a business setting, that concern for morality is not expected. In addition, the myth holds that "businesses act immorally not because of a desire to do evil, but simply because they want to make a profit and therefore disregard some of the consequences of their actions."[1] What we are seeing in the negative perception of business is the breakdown of this myth.

According to De George this breakdown has been signaled in three ways. *First,* there are those reports of and reactions to corporate scandals. *Second,* there has been a rise in the number of groups whose purpose is to promote and support the views of consumerists, environmentalists, and other public interest bodies. *Finally,* business itself is showing concern for social issues.

The growing acceptance of the existence of a relation between business and morality is yet another indication of the decline of the myth of amoral business. De George focuses on five factors which highlight this relationship between business and morality. *First,* business is part of society, not something separate and imposed upon it. Business activity is human activity and, therefore, can be evaluated from the moral point of view just as any other human activity can be. In addition, there is, as in other social activities, a presupposition of a background of morality. For example, honesty and truthfulness are taken for granted in the marketplace. Employers do not expect their employees to steal from them; signatories to a contract expect each other to honor its conditions. This does not mean that there are no immoral actions in the business sphere. It does mean that those actions take place within a moral context. As De George points out, "There is no proof that people are more immoral in their business lives than in their private lives. The structures of business are no more prone to immorality than the structures of government, family, education, or religion."[2]

A *second* factor, often ignored in assessing the relation of business and morality, is that the business of business is determined by the society in which it exists. The mandate to do business is given by society which determines what practices are or are not tolerable and sets limits indicating what is or is not proper activity. This determination of "what the business of business is, in fact, is itself a moral decision and one that is socially made and implemented."[3]

A *third* factor which must be taken into account when considering the relationship between business and morality is the place of law. According to De George:

> The dissociation of management from ownership took place at the same time that laws regulating business proliferated. As a result, it was natural for those who were managing firms, to feel that what society and stockholders of their company required of them was compliance with the law. If they complied with the law, they fulfilled their social obligations. As a result, they began to feel that morality was personal, that it varied from person to person and from group to group, and that all that could be expected of the managers of business, as well as of business itself, was fulfillment of the law.[4]

In De George's view this provided a justification for ignoring moral demands and enhanced the myth of amoral business. He feels that "the retreat to law as the sole norm by which to guide business is in part a reflection of the fact that most managers do not know how to handle many moral issues in business."[5] It does not mean that business and morality are unrelated.

A *fourth* factor to be considered is the changing mandate for business emerging in the United States. The more general mandate to supply quality goods and services at the lowest possible price is being modified. Society's demands on business are more complex and are often conflicting ones. There is a growing awareness that many actions in the economic sphere involve value judgments. One of the problems that this highlights, according to De George, is the fact that firms often lack internal structures necessary to weigh various demands and deal with moral as well as financial considerations.

The *final* factor which De George mentions is the question of property. The type of ownership, public or private, and the rights governing ownership of property reflect the attitudes and customs of a given society. He makes it clear that questions about property and the right to use or own property, including such things as natural resources, are not economic ones but social ones. Sometimes these rights are governed by laws which identify and protect rights of ownership. But even here, De George cautions, laws might at times be insufficient and more basic moral rights governing the use of certain property might have to be considered.

From De George's perspective these five factors suggest that business and morality are not mutually exclusive. The myth of amoral business might have allowed people to ignore the interdependency of business and morality. However, De George believes that as the myth is further exploded the depth of the relationship between business and morality will become even more apparent.

Already this is seen in the emerging realization on the part of business that it is not structured to deal with questions of values and morality. Coupled with this, De George notes that most managers have had little, if any, training in developing skills needed to integrate moral views into the decision-making process.[6] Businesses, beginning to feel the need to respond to social issues, are realizing that they lack the means to do so effectively. To overcome this deficiency, firms are becoming increasingly involved in employee training, social audits, codes of practice, and other measures in an effort to better prepare managers to deal with non-quantitative social issues in the decision-making process.

The Place and Meaning of Eucharist in the Life of Faith

I would like to address these issues from the perspective of membership in the faith community in an effort to discover how participation in the life of that community, particularly participation in the Eucharist, impacts and shapes responses to ethical dilemmas. While not intending to present an in-depth discussion of the theology of the Eucharist, it is, nevertheless, important to the task at hand to have some understanding of the place and meaning the Eucharist should have in the life of all of us who participate in it. The Eucharistic celebration is at the center of the Church's public worship. Participation in the Eucharist signifies the totality of Christian existence. It is in Christ that the answer to the meaning of existence is given ultimate clarity. He is the model of all perfection, of full human personhood. Through his death and resurrection he has liberated humankind from sin and brought a new freedom to human existence. It is a freedom to respond positively to God's self-gift of love, through Christ in the Spirit.

In the table-fellowship of the Eucharist, we encounter Christ present in the Word, in the bread and wine, and in all those who share in them. When we join in the public worship of the community at Mass, we actively participate in the mystery of God and the life of God's people. This participation identifies us as followers in Christ's footsteps and responders to his loving call—a call to be fully human.

The structure of the Mass highlights this experience. The introductory rites call us together as a community. They raise our awareness of our own humanity and help us to be open to the meaning of the celebration in which we participate. The proclamation of the Word follows. Here we are called to listen actively to the voice of God. This is not so much a discovery of what truths ancient texts might contain; rather, it is experiencing the communication of God's truth in a way which dynamically interacts with the present. Ideally, this interaction is brought into focus in the homily which is concerned with applying the Word of God to the everyday life of the worshiping community. The dynamic includes our listening to God's voice, understanding its demands in our lives, and responding to it. Within the structure of the Mass, this response comes in the liturgy of the Eucharist.

When we partake of the Eucharistic bread and wine, we are brought into intimate relation with God and each other in the unity of God's love. The inter-personal relationship arising from God's love for us, a love which we freely accept, places a two-fold obligation upon us. As members of the worshiping community we are called to be open to continual conversion in our life-long effort to reach full human personhood. Likewise, participation in the unity of God's love requires that the two great commandments which form the ethical base of life—love of God and love of neighbor—be taken seriously and be wholly incorporated in our lives.

Love of God forms us, as a Eucharistic people, into God's instruments. Thus, we should be willing to dedicate our lives to God's service and to bear witness to and preach the good news of salvation, the presence of God in the world, and the final coming of the reign of God. The service nature of this commitment is underscored in the concluding rite of the Mass as we are sent forth to love and serve God in the world. Participation in the Eucharist should free us from self-centered concerns and allow us to turn toward others with a loving attitude. By so doing we see Christ in all with whom we come in contact and fulfill the commandment to love our neighbor. In the spirit of true Christian love, we are called upon to actively assist others in their efforts to come to full human personhood. In each and every situation, other persons should be served in a way which acknowledges their human dignity and accords them the justice of which they are worthy.

The acceptance of this call to serve others will manifest itself in as many varied forms as there are situations and experiences in daily life. As we participate in the mystery of God's love in the Eucharist, we are called to create an atmosphere which will foster human growth and potential so that all may have the opportunity to encounter God. Often this takes place in interactions within our families or communities, though it is not limited to these relationships. The imperative to love—an imperative to which individuals bind themselves by free engagement in the Eucharist—is not a restrictive one but an all encompassing one. Thus, we are bound to care for and be concerned with the whole of humanity. As a Eucharistic people we must strive to further the coming of God's reign by acknowledging the dignity of each and every person and by bearing witness to the active presence of God in the world.

Responding in the Workplace

The question before us, therefore, is how participation in furthering the reign of God manifests itself in the workplace. I believe that our response to the ethical imperative of the Eucharist parallels the two-pronged approach mentioned earlier. We are not only to be concerned with the personal nature of the ethical imperative—that is, that we ourselves act with moral integrity; we are also to be concerned with the social or corporate dimension of our actions. In the workplace this means being concerned with establishing an environment that allows ethical reflection to be integrated into the managerial decision-making process.

The shape of the personal, or individual, response is not difficult to see. Whatever position an individual has and whatever task he or she performs must be done in a way that acknowledges and respects the human dignity of coworkers as well as those who are impacted by the individual's work. The commitment made through active participation in the Eucharist is not one that we leave at home or that only affects our private lives. We are called to actively promote the reign of God wherever we are. There are those who do not make this connection, who do not necessarily understand participation in the Eucharist in this way. Those persons who do not see the Mass as a communal activity that forms and identifies participants but see it as a priestly ritual to be observed will be less able to accept and act upon the ethical imperative of the Eucharist.

While I do not want to dwell on this issue, it is important to be aware of the limitations that it brings forth. It is also important to acknowledge the need to strive for a better understanding of the Eucharist and its central position in the life of the community. In this way we might be better able to recognize and appreciate the formative nature of the community's public worship and its imperative to love and serve others. To be clear, this is not to say that if only we understood and accepted the ethical imperative of the Eucharist and based our lives and actions on the two great commandments, all would be well in the world in general and the workplace in particular. That is too simplistic a view. The issues are more complex and go beyond the moral integrity of particular individuals. Individual morality is necessary and important but somehow it must transcend itself and move toward the creation of an environment which allows serious consideration to be given to ethical issues in the workplace.

If we take seriously the ethical imperative of the Eucharist as it relates to the workplace, then we should become involved in this process. This should not be an idea that is foreign to us. The whole tradition of Catholic social thought has been concerned with the way in which society is structured and with our participation in those structures. But what does this actually mean in terms of trying to integrate ethical reflection into the decision-making process and the day-to-day activities of the men and women who are responsible for our business enterprises? First, it means being concerned with and involved in individual moral development. Second, it means being concerned with the structure of the business enterprise itself so that it is designed in a way that allows ethical reflection to be an integral part of the decision-making process.

One of the important tasks on the individual level is to assist people in understanding and identifying those moral principles upon which their actions are based. This is particularly important if there are to be any substantive changes in the way in which managerial decisions are made. If I don't know where I stand and what principles guide my actions, I am not going to be very effective in making ethical reflection a part of the decision-making process. In addition, I will not be able to adequately assess the decisions of others and support or challenge them as is appropriate. The ability to assess different courses of action from a moral standpoint as well as a business standpoint is essential to making ethical reflection part of the decision-making process. There is a growing body of literature which attempts to assist managers and future managers in this task.

On the academic level this is done by introducing an ethics component to all business courses or by offering separate business ethics courses. In North America alone, nearly five hundred institutions of higher learning offer at least one course in business ethics. These focus on the institutional arrangements, policies, corporate politics, and the social ethos of business decision making and action. The courses attempt to provide students with sufficient knowledge to enable them to approach moral issues intelligently and to enter into the ongoing debate on the morality of certain business practices. In addition, the courses try to assist students in identifying and moving toward developing structures that foster individual acceptance of moral responsibility and fulfillment of moral obligations.

On a more practical level there has been an upsurge in "how to" books as well as an increase in special courses and other on-the-job training programs designed to help workers find solutions for difficult problems in business. These problems center around issues such as product safety, employment practices, occupational safety, pollution control, environmental protection, marketing strategies, truth in advertising, fraud, bribery, pricing policies, and foreign investment practices. The current demand is for a framework which managers can use to bring ethical reflection into the decision-making process. Different authors and researchers offer different methods. One of these, *Values and Ethics in Organization and Human Systems Development* by Gellermann, Frankel, and Ladenson contains a five step model which provides managers with a systematic way of thinking and addressing problems. Gellermann, who proposed the model, stated that his

> purpose in describing the model is to encourage ethical sensitivity, thought, and action in real situations. Though easily expressed, this idea needs fuller explanation.
> First, the model is intended as a tool for use in:
> - Increasing *sensitivity* to situations that require ethical thought and action
> - Developing *ability to think* about possibilities for ethical action
> - Developing *ability to act* in ways consistent with thinking (namely actions that yield consequences consistent with one's values and ethics)
>
> Second, ability to think about ethical problems can be thought of as a matter of "fluency" analogous to fluency in use of language, since it literally involves conversation with one's self. The smoothness with which that dialogue flows is fundamental to making decisions based on understanding and commitment rather than on mere compliance.[7]

The process which Gellermann proposes should sound familiar to those conversant with modern Catholic social thought whose centenary we are celebrating. This same type of process was put forth by Pope John XXIII. In the fourth section of *Mater et magistra,* he shows his concern with the reconstruction of social relationships through the norms of truth, justice, and love. He notes that justice and peace cannot exist if human beings are unwilling to recognize their dignity and accept that they are "necessarily the foundation, cause, and end of all social institutions" (MM 219). Among the obstacles leading to this unwillingness is an instinctive and immoderate self-interest coupled with a materialistic bent that makes it "difficult to discern the demands of justice in a given situation" (MM 229).

From John XXIII's perspective, it is not sufficient to present the social teachings of the Church to people. They must also be shown how these teachings can be applied. This is done in three stages:

> First, the actual situation is examined; then, the situation is evaluated carefully in relation to these teachings; then only is it decided what can and should be done in order that the traditional norms may be adapted to circumstances of time and place. These three steps are at times expressed by the three words: *observe, judge, act* (MM 236).

John XXIII readily acknowledged that differing views as to what constitutes appropriate action will arise. In these cases, the extent to which agreement can be reached and cooperation can take place should be examined in a mutually respectful manner. It is necessary to be consistent and uncompromising in situations which would impinged on moral or religious integrity. In addition, he warned against allowing personal interests to overshadow judgments. John XXIII also issued a challenge which is still valid today and has been repeated by Pope Paul VI and Pope John Paul II. He challenged all of us to take seriously our responsibility for action in the world and to insure that we are qualified and properly educated so that we can undertake our professional tasks suitably and in a manner that conforms to the teachings and norms of the Church.

Meeting that challenge in the workplace requires that we be persons of moral integrity. This will tend to alleviate some of the more basic and easily identifiable problems in the business sphere. Among these are insider trading, fraud, graft, and other types of dishonest behavior. But that is not enough. We must also be able to find a way to integrate ethical reflection in the managerial decision-making process without ignoring the complexities of the business world and the competing interests that are found in it. This means creating models of decision making which allow the identification of values and assumptions upon which decisions and policies are based. Once these values and assumptions are identified, the task is to determine their adequacy. The moral principles set out in the social teaching and the concept of justice which those principles support can provide the norms for assessing the adequacy of particular actions. In this way we can begin to respond to the ethical imperative arising from active participation in the Eucharist. We will be taking seriously our responsibility for creating a better world by participating in its transformation in our own particular circumstances.

Notes

[1] Richard De George, *Business Ethics* (New York: Macmillan, 1986) 4.
[2] De George, 9.
[3] De George, 11.
[4] De George, 11.
[5] De George, 12.
[6] De George, 5.
[7] William Gellermann, Mark S. Frankel, and Robert F. Ladenson, *Values and Ethics in Organization and Human Systems Development* (San Francisco: Jossey-Bass, 1990) 64.

7
Poverty and Prosperity in Global Economics: Making Sense of Conflicting Claims

Daniel Rush Finn

A wise man once said, "Nothing is as simple as most people think it is." While this may not always be true, it certainly applies to the economic development of the Third World. The reasons for this are several.

The formulation of good economic policies, even for the United States or other developed countries, is a complex business involving differing economic analyses and diverse values. Any attempt to propose good economic policies for the developing world is made considerably more difficult by the immense poverty which enfolds the majority there and by the gulf which exists between the alternative explanations for that impoverishment. While critics on the left accuse international capitalism of sustaining this destitution, analysts from the right praise the free market future as the only real hope for ending it.

Roman Catholic social thought has attempted to analyze the moral issues implicit in such economic questions. Pope John Paul II's encyclical *Centesimus annus* has addressed these issues helpfully, but as with earlier Church documents, people on both sides of the issue claim that it supports their own views and criticizes those of the opposition. The current debate among Christians about economic life in the Third World is filled with disagreements. There are many different perspectives, but we shall focus on two: liberation theology, as represented by Gustavo Gutierrez, and the neoconservative defense of democratic capitalism, represented by Michael Novak.

We shall try to establish a sort of dialogue between these two positions, even though the two sides are not regularly talking to each other. Both feel seriously misunderstood by the other and their disagreements are not easy to sort out. There is no neat resolution of their differences, but examining these two perspectives will lead to a better understanding of what is at stake.

Gustavo Gutierrez and Liberation Theology

Liberation theology begins with the assumption that people of faith already possess a rough outline of a theology, regardless of their educational level or their ability to articulate that theology. As Gustavo Gutierrez sees it, all Christians try to understand the faith. As a result, what professional theologians think and write about theology is a second step in the faith. The Christian community lives out the faith and develops an implicit theology by reflecting on it. The theologian is in a secondary position in the Church, not telling people what to believe but helping people articulate the truth in which they already participate in their daily life.

A second assumption of liberation theology is that when we ask *whose* faith is to be reflected upon, we should do as Jesus did: identify with the poor. Gutierrez would say that if we want to understand Christian faith, particularly in a Third World country, we need to be with the people who are living out the Christian faith. We need to work with the poor, who are trying to embody responsibly the Christian faith in their own concrete attitudes and activities. We need to be with people who are trying to make the Gospel alive in their own life, in their village, in their area of the countryside.

The Word of God that comes to the poor in Christian faith is a word of liberation. Jesus brought a message to the poor, outcasts and sinners: God wants them to live a full and liberated life. But this theme of religious liberation was not a novelty with Jesus. As Gutierrez points out, the God of the Hebrew Scriptures is a liberating God. That most fundamental of all events in the history of Israel—the Exodus—was a clear act of liberation of the people by Yahweh. And it was not simply an other-worldly liberation but a political as well as spiritual liberation for God's people. Much more can and is said about this notion of liberation, but the point is that, from the perspective of Latin American liberation theology, the theologian's task is to reflect on the liberating activity of Christian people attempting to free themselves from their oppression.

Gutierrez claims that liberation occurs on three "levels." First, there is economic, and political liberation; this is the level most frequently referred to by the press in their descriptions of liberation theology. This type of liberation ranges from the development of informal cooperation in rural villages to organization of producer co-ops to participation in national efforts to establish democratic political parties and constitutions. The second level of liberation is a longer term liberation in history. This includes the awareness that what the poor and oppressed do today stands not simply on its own but is a part of a long-term historical effort of humanity to move toward greater liberation. What is done today or even during our own lifetime has a larger meaning in the historical effort to bring about in a greater degree what God intends for the world. The third level entails liberation from sin and movement toward community with others and with God. Sin entails personal decisions; as Christians we are all personally sinful people. At the same time, it includes structural sin, the capacity for our institutions to perpetuate injustice and abuse. Liberation must include both the transformation of oppressive economic and political structures and the conversion of individual persons.

It is important to understand that Gutierrez's view here is of an integrated liberation. There is not one act that liberates economically and another that liberates from sin. Rather, a single act, even the simple meeting of a dozen poor people to begin talking about establishing a producer co-op in their village, is an effort at liberation at all three levels. It is an act against sinfulness in the world and a part of the historical effort at liberation as well as this concrete attempt to improve the economic lives of this village.

The role of base communities (*communidades de base*) is critical in this process. All over Latin America there are tens of thousands of common people who gather in small groups to read the Scriptures and to reflect on their meaning in their lives. It is a fundamental assumption of liberation theology that people gather to make the liberating word of the Gospel more alive in their local situation, praying, reading and acting. This integration between liturgy, prayer, and social activity is fundamental to liberation theology.

Gutierrez, like other liberation theologians, does not say much about economic theory, but it is clear that he endorses socialism:

> Latin American nations should change from the capitalistic mode of production to the socialistic mode, that is to say, to one oriented towards a society in which people can begin to live freely and humanly.[1]

Liberation theologians in general have little to recommend about the particular form that should be taken by socialism, though they do indicate it should be a thoroughly democratic and decentralized socialism, one quite different from that typified for so long in the Soviet Union. The fundamental conviction here is that the influence of large corporations from the United States and other industrialized countries has had severely negative effects in Third World countries. In this, of course, liberation theologians are not alone. As Pope John Paul II said in *Centesimus annus:*

> Many formerly colonized nations find that decisive sectors of the economy still remain de facto in the hands of large foreign companies which are unwilling to commit themselves to the long-term development of the host country. Political life itself is controlled by foreign powers.[2]

Both liberation theologians and the Pope are concerned that the endorsement of self-interest in capitalism often allows individuals and firms to act in destructive ways.

Michael Novak and Democratic Capitalism

The second major perspective to be considered in this essay is that presented by Michael Novak, a well-known theologian who has been writing on economic topics over the last two decades. From his perspective:

> It is not those who say "The Poor! The Poor!" who will enter the Kingdom of Heaven, but those who actually put in place an economic system that helps the poor no longer to be poor.[3]

Novak argues that for all its concern about altruism and for all its suspicion of self-interest, the Church should not be criticizing democratic capitalism. It is that system, he asserts, which has actually helped poor people more than any other. He argues that the Churches, particularly the Roman Catholic Church, have not been appreciative enough of the insights embodied in democratic capitalism.

Novak's hope is that the prosperity experienced by immigrants to the United States over the past century can belong to the poor of the Third World. Our immigrant forbears, he reminds us, came to this nation and built an economic prosperity not by cutthroat, dog-eat-dog exploitation of neighbor, but by founding a local grocery store or dairy farm or other business aimed at serving other people. A system that allows hard working people to get ahead is one which will help the poor most.

Novak contends that the best structure for assisting the poor of the Third World is that of democratic capitalism, comprising a political system, an economic system, and a moral/cultural system. Each of these must have a kind of relative autonomy, with the moral/cultural system providing the values and socialization of individuals that allow for a humane world. Such a system, he argues, has led to numerous inventions, including intellectual devices, that have made for prosperity for even impoverished immigrants. Among these inventions are joint stock companies, which allow for the formation of corporations even by people without great wealth. In this view the traditions of budgeting and accounting and watching the bottom line are not bad; they detect when resources are being wasted. A banking system where credit is available for everyone and not just the rich does much to assist the poor. The legal protection of inventions and other sorts of intellectual property through trademarks and copyrights are critical for prosperity.

Novak's message for Church leaders is that they should spend more time worrying about their own role in the moral/cultural sphere than they do about politics and economics. Thus, from his perspective, liturgy as an instrument of social justice must focus on the development of just individuals and communities who act virtuously within a relatively free market.

The vision which Novak offers for the Third World is based on his view of the prosperity of many East Asian nations, such as Hong

Kong, Singapore, Korea, and Japan. Wealth, he says, wells up from the bottom and does not trickle down. In Hong Kong in 1980, he points out, twenty thousand factories employed fewer than ten persons. These are factories making products we have all purchased: shoes, shirts, other consumer products. Only forty factories in all of Hong Kong employed more than a thousand people. The cost of opening a small business was about $30.00 in United States money, meaning that one need not be wealthy to start a business there. This type of small-scale prosperity provided within democratic capitalism is his hope for Latin America and the rest of the Third World. Capitalism, not socialism, is the way to go. The key here is incentives:

> Society should offer persons of imagination and enterprise social incentives for abstaining from consumption, for venturing what they have, and for putting the underemployed to gainful and productive work.[4]

A Constructive Dialogue

Of course, the debate between Gutierrez and Novak has roots as old as humanity itself. Certainly the doctrine of creation, both as understood in the Hebrew Scriptures and as developed in later Christian theology, means that those who own property can only own it in a limited way because it belongs most fundamentally to God. In fact, the gift which God made of the earth to all human beings is a fundamental part of the Christian view of property. As St. Ambrose of Milan taught 1600 years ago:

> Not from your own do you bestow upon the poor man but you make return from what is his. For what has been given as common for the use of all, you appropriate to yourself alone. The earth belongs to all, not to the rich . . . Therefore you are paying a debt, you are not bestowing what is not due.[5]

Throughout our history, from the Deuteronomic restrictions on harvesting to the medieval Thomistic analysis of property ownership as entailing "common use," the tradition has always specified restrictions on the powers of ownership. It has placed private ownership by the wealthy in service to the poor who do not have the necessities of life. It is exactly this claim which all persons have on creation that leads Pope John Paul II to assert that "the State must ensure in every case the necessary minimum support for the unemployed worker."[6] This is not laissez-faire economics.

Catholic social thought has shown not only a growing clarity of critique against the abuses of both free market capitalism and totalitarian socialism, but also an increased appreciation for strengths of the market. As Pope John Paul has said:

> It would appear that, on the level of individual nations and of international relations, the free market is the most effective instrument for utilizing resources and effectively responding to needs.[7]

Conservative newspaper columnists have quoted this sentence many times and it does indeed express a strong appreciation for markets. However, the same Pope also acknowledges that ". . . there are many human needs that find no place on the market. It is a strict duty of justice and truth not to allow fundamental human needs to remain unsatisfied. . . ."[8] These principles of Catholic social thought must be applied to the Third World.

On the one hand, there is a positive appreciation for the economic activity of individuals within the business system: "Profit has a legitimate role as an indication that a business is functioning well."[9] Thus, a firm is endorsed in its profit making as long as it also attends to other human values such as the existence of a community of persons which make up the business. Similarly, the activity of entrepreneuers is itself a positive economic contribution:

> The ability to forsee both the needs of others and the combinations of productive factors most adapted to satisfying those needs constitutes an important source of wealth. Initiative and entrepreneurial ability is an essential part of disciplined and creative human work.[10]

On the other hand, the current Pope and the long tradition of Roman Catholic social teaching have held that even though a limited autonomy is allowed to firms in economic life:

> The State, however, has the task of determining the juridical framework within which economic affairs are to be conducted, and thus, of safeguarding the prerequisites of a free economy,

which presumes a certain equality between the parties, such that one party would not be so powerful as practically to reduce the other to subservience.[11]

If we stand back and look at the argument between Gutierrez and Novak in light of the Pope's most recent teaching, there are a number of observations we might make. Learning from Novak, we observe that much of the abuse which the poor and oppressed in the Third World experience comes not simply from the nature of a market system. Much of it arises from a centuries old social structure where the elites in Third World countries live in prosperity and enjoy privileges that have long pre-dated the arrival of American multi-nationals or even the market system.

Learning from Gustavo Gutierrez, the neo-conservative position illustrates a kind of astigmatism in its focus on the free initiative of individuals and its blindness to what the Pope has called the "juridical structure" within which markets operate. By this the Pope means that vast array of legal structures and procedures which does everything from defining the rights of property owners to providing for the needs of the weakest members of society. We know that children labored in the mills and mines of England one hundred and fifty years ago, before there were any laws about child labor. The free market by itself would never have put an end to this activity. Rather, it was governmental decision that outlawed this and numerous other abusive practices. In fact, it is only when the moral "floor" is raised that well-meaning entrepreneurs no longer have to worry about competing with their unethical rivals (who *would* resort to the hiring of children if it were legal). Time and again abusive behavior has been outlawed, thus allowing for a more humane version of democratic capitalism. Many of the debates are not about whether we should allow markets, but rather about what restrictions we should impose before allowing markets to operate relatively freely.

This insight leads us to an interpretation of self-interest within Christian social ethics. The historic concern for the love of neighbor has left Christians without a clear theological stance on self-interest. Jesus' mandate that the disciple offer a tunic to the robber who would have stolen only the cloak has not encouraged a careful theological articulation of self-interest in the tradition. To understand some of the complexity, consider an example.

When any of us goes to the grocery store, we look over the produce, say, looking for a cantaloupe, in order to choose the best one we can find. The more altrusitic action would, of course, be to choose the worst looking one. This would allow a better choice for those who come after us. But it is no shame to seek out the best cantaloupe. This act of self-interest is not abusive, because the power distributed among the various shoppers in the grocery is approximately equal and we do no great harm when we look out for ourselves there. In fact, the grocer upon finding only rotten cantaloupe left at the end of the week will have an incentive to find the stock clerks who may have bruised the fruit. Or the grocer may turn to the wholesaler and threaten to buy from a different source if more care is not taken with the produce. All along the line, the self-interest of each of those in the food chain may then lead to a more responsible use of the resources of the earth.

On the other hand, as we move to the next aisle in the grocery to buy a pound of coffee our self-interest may in fact be destructive. There we do not choose the best bag of coffee but rather choose one of a number of identical bags. The issue here is not the relative power between consumers in this grocery but the effects caused in the Third World by our drinking coffee. It is a fact of economics that the overall demand for coffee has raised the price of the best farm land in coffee-producing nations in the Third World, leaving the poor of those nations unable to own or rent land that they might otherwise use for growing local grains to feed themselves. There is no simple solution here; abstaining from coffee (or bananas or cocoa or other imports) won't do it. The point is that a simple reliance on the free market is just that—too simple.

In summary, our consideration of liberation theology and neoconservative capitalism *can* find some common ground. Both sides endorse the economic activity of the poor. Both sides believe that all persons in society should be able to play a productive part in the economy and thereby support themselves and their families. There remain, however, huge differences between the two positions concerning the effects of large corporations, with liberation theologians highly critical and conservatives generally appreciative of their impact in the Third World.

Still, there is ground for common conversation proposed by Roman Catholic social thought. The Church needs a lively debate regarding the content of a juridical structure within which markets and the self-interests of individuals could effectively operate. The debate ought not to be understood as asking whether the government should "intervene" in the market, for this ignores the current juridical structure; rather, it is about the structures which such communal decisions would insist upon prior to allowing the free play of interest to occur. This does not by any means solve the problems of wealth and poverty in the Third World, but it does offer us a helpful framework.

Notes

[1] Gustavo Gutierrez, *A Theology of Liberation* (Maryknoll, N.Y.: Orbis, 1973) 30.

[2] John Paul II, *Centesimus annus (On the Hundredth Anniversary of Rerum novarum)* U.S.C.C. edition, sect. 20, 41.

[3] Michael Novak, *Will It Liberate?* (Mahweh, N.J.: Paulist, 1986) 125.

[4] M. Novak, *Will It Liberate?*, 122.

[5] Ambrose of Milan, *De Nabuthe*, 11 *Patralogia Latina* 14:747.

[6] John Paul II, *Centesimus annus*, sect. 15, 33.

[7] John Paul II, *Centesimus annus*, sect. 34, 66.

[8] John Paul II, *Centesimus annus*, sect. 34, 67.

[9] John Paul II, *Centesimus annus*, sect. 35, 68.

[10] John Paul II, *Centesimus annus*, sect. 32, 62.

[11] John Paul II, *Centisimus annus*, sect. 15, 31.

8

God's Creation and the Christian's Response

Bernard F. Evans

They all look to you, Lord,
   to give them food in due time.
When you give it to them, they gather it;
   when you open your hand,
   they are filled with good things.
If you hide your face, they are dismayed;
   if you take away their breath,
   they perish and return to their dust.
When you send forth your spirit,
   they are created,
   and you renew the face of the earth (Ps 104:27-30).

Psalm 104 is a beautiful and humbling hymn of praise to the Creator. It acknowledges our absolute dependence upon God for life and for everything needed to sustain that life. It reminds us that there is very little we human beings can add to the wonderful, resilient, coherent world that God alone has created. We are not, despite the wonders of modern technology, makers and creators of the world we inhabit.

As we respond to all of God's loving actions, so also we respond to God's creation—with love and reverence, with thanksgiving, with actions of respect for the earth and of justice for our neighbors. Psalm 104, this hymn of praise, is surrounded by psalms of thanksgiving for God's covenant faithfulness and righteousness. Together these psalms remind us that our response to God's creation and specifically our attention to environmental problems of the day must be formed by liturgy and social justice.

Our Christian heritage—that developing source of religious, spiritual, and ethical wisdom—provides fundamental insights on how we might shape our response to God's creation. In that heritage we may find as well the guidance needed for responding to the present-day environmental crisis.

In making this claim I recognize that this direction, this guidance, does not come in the form of specific guidelines. Indeed the "environment" is rarely mentioned in Christian sources and when it is, the natural world of plants and animals and land and water often appears in a position of subordinance to human beings. And yet, within our religious heritage there is an attitude or spirit towards creation which can inform our hearts, habits, and daily actions.

This essay discusses certain aspects of that spirit or attitude towards creation which is present in our Christian heritage. I wish to focus on those aspects which I believe can bring a needed perspective into contemporary discussions regarding environmental problems. Second, I will explore how that spirit or attitude towards creation can be present in our liturgical celebrations and thereby influence our daily lives.

Christian heritage

The biblical sources of our religious and theological heritage provide challenges for the Christian's response to God's creation. To some readers of the Old Testament, the Bible seems to justify human exploitation and destruction of the natural world. I refer especially to the ongoing debate about whether the Bible is too anthropocentric in its world view.[1] That debate is fueled by such biblical passages as the Genesis creation account in which human beings are given "dominion over the fish of the sea, the birds of the air, and all living things that move on the earth" (Gen 1:28).

These same biblical sources, however, provide other insights regarding our relationship to creation—a relationship that is not one of master and servant, of human beings having dominion over the natural world in a hierarchical and utilitarian sense. A glimpse of that relationship is found in the Old Testament's discussion of Israel's relationship to the land, as well as in the New Testament's claim that all of creation is renewed in Christ. These themes, along with some from Catholic social teaching, offer the material for this brief examination of our Christian heritage's guidance on environmental issues.

Old Testament

The Old Testament Sabbath tradition is quite familiar. Among its many prescriptions was a required time of rest not only for human beings, but also for the land itself, as well as for periodic redistribution of land ownership. Richard Austin notes that in this tradition we find a biblical ecology that supports the liberation of both people and land from oppression.[2]

Exodus 23 prescribes this year of rest for the land every seventh year. Its purpose was both to rest the land and to assure access to food for the poor and wild animals:

> For six years you may sow your land
>   and gather in its produce.
> But the seventh year you shall let the land lie
>   untilled and unharvested
> that the poor among you may eat of it
>   and the beasts of the field
>   may eat what the poor leave.
> So also shall you do in regard to your
>   vineyard and your olive grove (Exod 23:10-11).

The Sabbath law here is concerned with rules and regulations that go beyond farming and caring for the land. They are above all principles to control greed. These principles provide us with insights on how we are to respond to God's creation, how we are to relate to the natural world, and what our selfish inclinations should not allow us to do to God's good earth. The message in these texts is simple and clear: the land commands respect.

The Book of Leviticus reminds us that during the seventh year "the land shall have a complete rest, a sabbath for the Lord" (Lev 25:4). Later, in chapter 26 we read how the Lord will enforce the rights of the land when these rights are not respected by an abusive people.

> You yourselves I will scatter among the nations
>   at the point of my drawn sword,

> leaving your countryside desolate
>   and your cities deserted.
> Then shall the land retrieve its lost sabbaths
>   during all the time it lies waste,
> while you are in the land of your enemies;
>   then shall the land have rest
> and make up for its sabbaths,
>   during all the time it lies desolate,
> enjoying the rest that you would not let it have
>   on the sabbaths when you lived there (Lev 26:33-35).

The land, and all of God's creation, is to be treated with dignity and respect. If an abusive people cannot understand this, then perhaps the Creator will have to remind us that the natural world is not here simply to serve human beings, but also to praise its Creator. It has that purpose; it has that right.

Our relationship to the land, to the larger environment, is closely connected to our relationship with our neighbor, a lesson often ignored in contemporary environmental debates. The Scriptures speak of a relationship between the fertility of the land and justice among people. When proper relationships exist between the land and its people, among the people living upon the land, and between the people and their God, then one could expect the land to bring forth abundant harvests, as we read in Psalm 85:

> Love and fidelity have come together;
>   justice and peace join hands.
> Fidelity springs up from the earth
>   and justice looks down from heaven.
> The Lord will add prosperity
>   and our land shall yield its harvest (Ps 85:11-13).

Fidelity, peace and justice among God's people make possible fertile soil, clear water and pure air. When people are oppressed or at war we know—as the Persian Gulf experience attests—that all of God's creation suffers. Fertility and bountiful harvests, and a restored healthy environment are impossible without justice to the land and to all who depend upon the land.

Biblical scholar Walter Brueggemann has written about the relationship between a healthy environment and justice among people. This relationship is seen especially in the Bible's related and parallel condemnations of land abuse and the abuse of women. When Israel regarded land and women as commodities to serve personal gain and satisfaction, the Bible condemned both practices as departures from the religious covenant understood in a communal sense. Notes Brueggemann:

> Sexuality and economics are the two great spheres of our life, the ones about which we most trouble, over which we most quarrel, and toward which we most hope. When sexuality is connected to fertility, and when economics is connected to justice, we are close to the core of all biblical ethics, for the Bible insists that fertility is impossible without justice. . . .[3]

In the experience of Israel, abuse of the land as well as the oppression of people, made fertile soil and rich harvests unlikely. Fidelity, peace and justice among God's people are the prerequisites for fertile land and an all-around healthy environment.

The history of our own nation should remind us that the destructive exploitation of the natural world does not occur without consequences for people, especially for those who are economically and politically vulnerable. The conquest of this land happened at enormous cost to Native Americans. Sprays used today to control insects in the California produce fields also threaten the health and lives of farmworkers. As the industrialization of American agriculture continues—often at high cost to soil and water—farm families and rural communities are cast aside as byproducts of an inevitable modernization process.

It is of little consequence that Israel, in all likelihood, did not enforce the Sabbath laws regarding the land. Rather, it is important that these precepts offered a moral framework to control human greed in a society in which land ownership concentration was always a threat, in a society in which the number of landless poor was very great, in a society very much like our own.

Our biblical heritage reminds us that responding to God's creation means respecting all of it. We cannot have a healthy environment without just relationships among people. Likewise, we cannot move significantly towards a more just society without respecting the place and the rights of the natural world in God's creative order.

New Testament

In his Letter to the Romans, Paul states that creation itself would be freed from corruption to share in "the glorious freedom of the children of God," that creation eagerly awaits the revelation and redemption of Christ (Rom 8:18-23). As the natural world was affected by the corruption brought on by human sin, so now it would somehow participate in the liberation from sin and death.

The New Testament should cause us to examine our attitude towards creation.[4] At the very least Paul reminds us that all of creation—not only human beings, but the entire created order—in some way was affected by Christ's redeeming act. If that is the case, then surely we must rethink our utilitarian and often abusive stance towards land, water, the air, and the animal world, as well.

As Christians, we view the universe as sacramental; the world reveals the presence of God through everyday happenings both great and small. Our worship and our sacraments draw from the natural world the tangible signs of God's activity in our lives. Bread and wine, oil and water—goods of creation are so important in our liturgy because they so powerfully remind us of God's saving presence in our lives, in the community, in the world.

The New Testament offers no direct comment upon what our relationship to the natural world should be, or upon our responsibilities to care for the land or to work for an environment capable of sustaining life on into the future. Nevertheless, the Gospels and the letters to the early Christian communities have much to say about love of neighbor and about moderation in our use and accumulation of material goods. If we remember the Old Testament linkage of our relationship to the land and our relationship to our neighbor, it is not difficult to appreciate these basic New Testament themes of love and moderation as bearing directly upon the Christian's response to God's creation.

Catholic Social Teaching

A third area of our Christian heritage to which we might turn in this search is Catholic social teachings. This body of teachings deserves mention because of a fairly recent interest on the part of the Church *magisterium* to address the environmental crisis.[5]

A century of Catholic social teaching has had very little to say about humankind's relationship to the natural world. When this teaching speaks of the created order or environmental topics, it inevitably views the natural world in a position of subordination to human beings. For example, the Second Vatican Council document The Pastoral Constitution on the Church in the Modern World offers many references to human beings as having "dominion" or "control" or "mastery" over the natural world.[6] More recently the United States Catholic Bishops' pastoral letter Economic Justice for All warns that we are to collaborate with the Creator in using the earth's resources to meet human needs both now and in the future.[7] With its focus upon the dignity of the human person, any discussion of creation without references to the human person has been difficult for Catholic social teaching.

Nevertheless, the encyclical tradition has developed a number of teachings which reflect the biblical themes already discussed. They include: the special place of human beings in God's creation; the absolute demand for justice, especially with regard to the poor and the vulnerable; the solidarity that should inform our relationships with people everywhere and that should restrain excessive desires for material accumulations. These are themes that run throughout Pope John Paul II's 1990 World Day of Peace message ("Peace with God the Creator, Peace with All of Creation"). They are found also in the 1991 United States Catholic Bishops' pastoral letter on the environment (Renewing the Earth: An Invitation to Reflection and Action on the Environment in Light of Catholic Social Teaching).

As noted earlier, issues of justice within the human community are often neglected in contemporary discussions on the environment. Pope John Paul II reminds us that "the proper ecological balance will not be found without directly addressing the structural forms of poverty that exist throughout the world."[8] Catholic social thought is not long on environmental statements, but its inclusion of justice issues within those statements may be the greatest contribution the Church's social teaching can bring to contemporary environmental debates.

Our Christian heritage offers directions for a human response to the environmental crisis, for it guides us in responding to God's creation. We must recognize, however, that this tradition has limits in what it can offer on this topic. Our biblical sources appear rather anthropocentric—rather focused upon the human—but even here contemporary biblical scholarship offers new insights well worth examining.[9] While it also focuses upon the human person, Catholic social teaching nevertheless provides useful perspectives not found in contemporary environmental discussions.

As we look to our Christian heritage for insights on how to respond to the current environmental crisis, I believe three points should be noted:

a. *Creation is the work of God*
As human, as created beings, we are to relate to the natural world in the most respectful and reverential way we know—because this world is created by God, and it is good. To enjoy the gifts of land and water and a clean environment is to relate to them as fellow creatures. We remain ever grateful for all of creation upon which we depend for continued life and through which we worship and praise our Creator.

b. *Environmental responsibility is ours*
Ours is a special place within creation. We believe the Creator has given us a particular responsibility to care for this world. We do so not as destructive and domineering self-seekers, but as loving fellow creatures acting on behalf of the Creator. To do less is to destroy our environment and risk the continuation of life on earth, including our own.

c. *Justice and moderation must lead*
We must come to understand that justice among all people and moderation in our use of material goods are prerequisites to ensuring a healthy environment. Our concern for the poor is not in conflict with our concern for the planet. Actions on behalf of justice and moderation in our use of the earth's resources are complimentary efforts to ensure a sustainable future in which everyone is assured the means to a dignified life.

Liturgical Implications

One of the great challenges facing a faith community is to allow our lives to reflect what our Christian heritage says about our response to God's creation. Surely one place where this teaching, this direction should take root is in our public worship—in those liturgical actions where we come together to praise and offer thanks, to set forth our needs, to express our faith and commit ourselves to action. How, then, do we make present in our liturgies, especially in our Eucharistic celebrations, those directives from our faith heritage that can move us to responsible actions on behalf of the environment? And, how do we do this without turning the liturgy into a "Christian Earth Day" or placing inappropriate and unreasonable expectations upon a parish community's celebration of the Eucharist?

Liturgy and Social Life

The liturgy does have a role to play in helping us make connections between our faith and our social life. This theme was often stressed by Fr. Virgil Michel, O.S.B. Through the liturgy we become aware of our responsibility to bring about change in this world, changes that will lead to a society and a world more characterized by charity and justice.[10]

The Eucharist in particular commits us as individuals and as a believing community to this task of transforming the world. The Second Vatican Council reminded us that our expectation of a new life does not take away our responsibility to build up this one.[11] Our communal celebration of the Eucharist is where we acknowledge our unity in Christ and where we commit ourselves to a life in harmony with the Kingdom of God. We must leave this celebration persuaded that changes are needed—in our personal lives, in our organized social life.

The Eucharist must never be simply an act of individual piety. It must create a community of people who together "unite prayer with action, praise with justice, adoration with transformation, and contemplation with social involvement."[12]

Pastoral Difficulties

And yet we well know how great is the pastoral challenge of preparing, presiding over, and participating in liturgies that empower us to such personal and worldly transformation. It is no less difficult, then, to experience in liturgical celebrations the movement and inspiration to responsible actions on behalf of the environment. Two reasons for this difficulty seem quite large.

The first is that we do not regularly make connections between our worship and our daily lives. Thus, we do not make the connection between worship and our response to God's creation because we are not in the habit of connecting liturgy and social life on an ordinary, daily basis. In a world of specialization, of narrowly defined functions and roles, we too often experience liturgy as a specialized activity or area of our lives unrelated to the whole. Msgr. Jack Egan writes that

> To the extent that liturgy is unconnected with daily life, it leads us either to a premature withdrawal from this world as beyond hope or to passive accomodation which confines love, peace and justice to church gatherings, but allows them no role in public life, in work, in economics, politics or culture."[13]

Egan argues that we cannot celebrate the story of God's love for us independent of our own stories without risking the absolute separation between faith and life.

If the relationship between liturgy and social justice is to become real, if the liturgy is to move us to responsible actions on behalf of the environment, then the liturgical actions of the people gathered to worship must reflect the life and characteristics of this particular community. The joys and hopes, the pain and despair found within our lives, the tension and conflict existing within our community are all aspects of the unfolding, living histories of who we are as a people. All of this is part of what we bring to the Eucharistic table and to all forms of communal prayer. If these regular happenings within our community's life are not, as a matter of course, expressed when the community gathers to worship, we should not expect larger social issues—like the environment—to be comfortably addressed in our celebrations.

A second difficulty in allowing the liturgy to inspire us to responsible actions on behalf of the environment is that of dealing with conflict. On the local level there is a strong reluctance to allow our public worship to remind us of sensitive and controversial issues, especially if these matters are rooted in the local community. If any issue holds the possibility of arousing dissagreement, conflict, or opposition, the local Church likely will ignore and avoid it altogether.

Today the environment is such an issue. If we move beyond recycling pop cans and begin asking more disturbing questions—about how our personal life styles contribute to the environmental crisis, about our nation's production and development policies, about the relationship between poverty and environmental degradation, about local farming practices—then we discover how uncomfortable and controversial this topic can become.

We need to learn how to deal creatively with tension and conflict in pastoral ministry. Until we do, the liturgy is not likely to express communal happenings about which there may be disagreement, tension, or conflict among the worshipers.

Worship: A Response to God's Creation

If the liturgy is to move us to responsible action on behalf of the environment, then the liturgical activities must regularly reflect the experiences of the parishioners. If the joys and sorrows of the people, both large and small happenings within the community, are not routinely expressed when the faithful gather to worship, it is little wonder that more difficult matters such as references to community problems or tensions, or larger social issues, are so rarely reflected in worship.

The use of symbols and art forms in the place of worship can be one step towards accomplishing that task. The atmosphere we create in the place of worship can be a way to keep the social aspect of liturgy before the communal consciousness of the parish. Appropriate art forms can constantly point to the reign of God as a tension between what is and what must be. In such an atmosphere what we celebrate in the liturgy necessarily beckons us to action after the liturgy.

One of the tasks of art, sanctuary furnishings and "liturgical environment" is to reflect the life and experience of this community. If this can be done regularly then the challenge to confront cultural norms which contribute to environmental degradation—a challenge which emanates from the liturgy itself—may not seem so foreign. If worshipers can see something of their ordinary, daily stories in the liturgical space, then perhaps it will seem less disturbing to be reminded of some larger issue, happening or problem in their lives—even one about which all don't agree.

A second way for the liturgy to move us to respond to God's creation is through the homily. If we are to develop the relationship between liturgy and social justice, if we are to allow the liturgy to move us to environmentally responsible actions, then we must talk about this during our celebration. One place for this to occur is the homily.

Clearly, it is not the place of the liturgy to impose moral imperatives and demand a particular course of action. The liturgy, nevertheless, does offer a call and a challenge to respond to needs in our world. The Eucharistic celebration in particular can make us more sharply aware of the disparity between the kind of community that should exist in God's creation and that which actually does.

To that end the homily should explain the Gospel and interpret the meaning of our lives in light of the Gospel. Walter Burghardt reminds us:

> It is this that must be preached—our fresh understanding of what the perennial gospel demands or suggests in the context of our time and space.[14]

That time and space necessarily includes a variety of small and large problems that are very much a part of everyday human living. That time and space for us today carries some fundamental, moral questions about how we respond to God's creation. Those questions inevitably raise points of tension and conflict.

In raising questions about God's creation, about today's environmental crisis, the homilist in fact is raising issues that are already part of the parish experience. It is not the task of the homilist to impose personal convictions as gospel, or to offer solutions to problems concerning which there are conflicting claims to justice. Rather, the task is to move worshipers to reflection upon their individual and communal experiences in light of the Gospel and the Eucharistic celebration. The homily cannot do this if it does not touch peoples' experiences. What is happening in the life of the parish community—all of this is possible reflection material for the homilist and the parishioners gathered around the altar.

Conclusion

Our Christian heritage challenges us to develop a sense of who we are in the created order. That heritage provides for relating to the natural world and for acting justly towards our sisters and brothers. We respect all of the created order because it is the work of God, and because without a healthy environment we cannot grow as human beings nor fully praise the God of the universe.

That spirit towards creation is present in our sacramental worship where elements of nature witness to God's presence in our lives. We gather as a Church to praise the Creator and to commit ourselves to building a world characterized by justice and an environment open to the renewing power of the Spirit.

Notes

[1] Dianne Bergant, C.S.A., "Is the Biblical Worldview Anthropocentric?" in *New Theology Review* 4 (May 1991); James Limburg, "Reflections on the Bible and the Care of the Earth" in *The Catholic World* (July/August 1990) 148–152; Bill McKibben, *The End of Nature* (New York: Random House, 1989); Lynn White, "The Historical Roots of Our Ecological Crisis," *Science* 155 (1967) 1203–1207.

[2] Richard Austin, "Rights for Life: Rebuilding Human Relationships with Land," *Theology of the Land,* Bernard F. Evans and Gregory D. Cusack, eds. (Collegeville: The Liturgical Press, 1987) 103–126.

[3] Walter Brueggemann, "Land: Fertility and Justice," *Theology of the Land,* Evans and Cusack, 42.

[4] Paulos Mar Gregorios, "New Testament Foundations for Understanding Creation," *Tending the Garden: Essays on the Gospel and the Earth* (Grand Rapids: Eerdmans, 1990) 83–92. In reflecting on New Testament principles for describing an appropriate relationship between humans and the rest of creation, Gregorios examines three New Testament texts: Rom 8:18-25, Col 1:15-23, and John 1:1-5.

[5] Especially noteworthy are the following documents: "Peace with God the Creator, Peace with All of Creation," Pope John Paul II's 1990 World Day of Peace message (Washington: United States Catholic Conference, Publishing Services, 1990) and "Renewing the Earth: An Invitation to Reflection and Action on the Environment in Light of Catholic Social Teaching," A Pastoral Statement of the United States Catholic Conference (Washington: U.S.C.C. Publishing Services, 1991).

[6] Pastoral Constitution on the Church in the Modern World, Second Vatican Council, 1965 (Washington: U.S.C.C. Publishing Services) nos. 9, 12, 15, 26, 33, 34, 53, 57, 63.